C. S. LEWIS

Creator of Narnia

C. S. LEWIS

CREATOR OF NARNIA

ELAINE MURRAY STONE

PAULIST PRESS
NEW YORK/MAHWAH, N.J.

Acknowledgments:
Autographed page on p. viii comes from *Surprised by Joy* by C. S. Lewis © 1955. First American edition 1956 by Harcourt Brace & Company, New York. Quotations from chapters 9 and 10 are from *A Grief Observed* by C. S. Lewis © 1961. Harper & Row, 1989, San Francisco. Originally published by Faber, London, 1961.

Cover art and interior illustrations by Patrick Kelley

Cover design by Faces Type & Design

Text copyright © 2001 by Dr. Elaine Murray Stone
Illustrations © 2001 by Patrick Kelley

Library of Congress Cataloging-in-Publication

Stone, Elaine Murray, 1922-
    C. S. Lewis : creator of Narnia / by Elaine Murray Stone ; illustrated by Patrick Kelley.
        p. cm.
    Includes bibliographical references.
    ISBN 0-8091-6672-0 (alk. paper)
        1. Lewis, C. S. (Clive Staples), 1898-1963. Chronicles of Narnia—Juvenile literature. 2. Lewis, C. S. (Clive Staples), 1898-1963—Juvenile literature. 3. Authors, English—20th century—Biography—Juvenile literature. 4. Children's stories, English—History and criticism—Juvenile literature. 5. Fantasy fiction, English—History and criticism—Juvenile literature. [1. Lewis, C. S. (Clive Staples), 1898-1963. 2. Authors, English.] I. Kelley, Patrick, 1963- ill. II. Title.

PR6023.E926 Z895 2001
823'.912—dc21
[B]

                                                                        2001021979

Published by Paulist Press
997 Macarthur Boulevard
Mahwah, New Jersey 07430

www.paulistpress.com

Printed and bound in the
United States of America

CONTENTS

This book is dedicated to my three daughters—

Catherine, Pamela, and Victoria

who grew up reading and loving the
Narnia books of C. S. Lewis

Lewis's autograph in the author's copy of
Surprised by Joy, *given to her by Lewis*
during a visit to his home in 1956.

Mr. & Mrs. Courtney-
- Stine
for
C. S. Lewis
13 / 5 / 56

PREFACE

In 1956 I was privileged to be the guest of C. S. Lewis in his home, "The Kilns," outside Oxford. Having been an avid reader of his books for years, I was thrilled to have this opportunity to talk with him over tea. But the famous religion writer was more interested in chatting with my late husband, F. Courtney Stone, an aerospace engineer at Cape Canaveral.

Professor Lewis asked Courtney about the latest advances in rocket and missile technology. Lewis was the author of a space trilogy and wanted to keep up with new techniques. We never did get around to religion that day, but Professor Lewis presented us with an autographed copy of his latest book, *Surprised by Joy*.

In 1998 I returned to Oxford and "The Kilns" for the centennial celebration of Lewis's birth, a two-week international symposium held at Oxford and Cambridge Universities sponsored by the C. S. Lewis Foundation of Redlands, California.

The daily sessions were held in the seventeenth-century Sheldonian Theater designed by Sir Christopher Wren. Each morning about six hundred delegates attended lectures by renowned theologians, scholars, and authors who had studied with Lewis. An added bonus were talks by his stepson, Douglas Gresham. The evenings were graced with special programs: a one-man show by actor Tom Key of Atlanta, Georgia, presenting "An Evening with C. S. Lewis"; a conversation on friendship acted by Newberry-award-winning author Madeleine L'Engle and her friend, poet/publisher Luci Shaw; selections from a new musical *Jack*, based on the life of Lewis, directed by the composer Keith Getty of Belfast, Northern Ireland; and an extraordinary world-premiere stage-play performance of *Till We Have Faces*, performed by the Lamb's Players of San Diego, California.

One afternoon was dedicated to the first-day issuance of a commemorative stamp by the British Royal Mail. The stamp portrayed the characters from Lewis's children's book *The Lion, the Witch, and the Wardrobe*. I was able to buy several commemorative stamps for my grandchildren, as well as a first-day cover autographed by Douglas Gresham.

Most surprising of the week's events was a tour of The Kilns given by Douglas, who lived there as a child and teenager. Now owned and recently renovated by the C. S. Lewis Foundation, the house looked completely different from the shabby, smoke-filled place I had visited in 1956, when Jack and his brother Warren lived there as bachelors.

After learning so much about Professor Lewis from the symposium, I wrote two articles about him and the centennial. After these were published, I was ready to write a book. Eight months later, I completed it. I hope it will bring a greater understanding of C. S. Lewis to young people who love his books about Narnia and want to know more about this very special author.

I would like to thank my editor, Susan O'Keefe, for her interest and support of my books, and Paulist Press for publishing them.

A special thanks to Dr. Stanley Mattson, founder and president of the C. S. Lewis Foundation, who directed Oxbridge '98, the wonderful centennial symposium at Oxford and Cambridge, and who added both keen insights and valuable facts to the manuscript. Also, I want to thank my typist and local editor, Cathy Rayburn, a devotee of Lewis since the age of seven. I particularly want to thank Douglas Gresham for all he shared about his childhood with his stepfather, C. S. Lewis, and his mother, Joy Gresham.

Elaine Murray Stone
Melbourne, Florida

CHAPTER ONE

BELFAST DAYS

"Jack, look what I made from an old biscuit tin," said Warren Lewis. Little Jack, his chubby face rosy with expectation, ran to the nursery door to see. (The famed author-to-be, baptized Clive Staples Lewis, had renamed himself "Jacksie" not long after he learned to talk.) His brother, nicknamed "Warnie," held out a used biscuit box that he had transformed into a miniature garden. Buried in the green moss lay tiny pebbles, blue forget-me-nots, pink primroses, and even a mirror to simulate a pond. Jack was entranced, and his older brother proud.

"May I hold it?" asked Jack timidly, not sure of the answer.

"Of course," replied Warnie, three years older than Jack. "I made it for Mother. But I wanted you to see it first."

At that moment, the children's Irish nurse, Lizzie Endicott, entered. She set down the boys' afternoon tea on a nearby table. Drawing Jack toward her, she asked sweetly, "What's this we have here?"

"Look, Lizzie," replied Jack. "Isn't this pretty? It's a tiny garden Warnie made for Mother. I wish I could do something that nice for her, too."

Lizzie brushed a brown lock from his eyes, "Now, me darling, don't pout," said the nurse. "And isn't it yourself that's colored her many a pretty picture? Elves and dressed-up rabbits. Why, many clever things. I know she is right proud of ye, Jackie, boy."

Lizzie ordered, "Come now. Sit down and have your tea. At the rate you boys tuck down biscuits, there'll soon be another tin for you, Jack."

"But," added Jack, "the garden was Warnie's idea. Mother will never think mine's as nice."

"Sure she will," nodded Lizzie, smiling.

Jack and Warnie were the privileged sons of an Irish attorney, Albert J. Lewis, and his beautiful wife, Flora. The Lewises lived in a large semiattached villa in Belfast, Northern Ireland. The villa had a moderate-sized garden with a part-time gardener to care for it. The boys' lives were well ordered, with morning lessons from their mother, who was a graduate in mathematics of Queen's College, Belfast. Later, Governess Harper instructed them in all other subjects.

Albert Lewis, their father, was of Welsh stock and the first in his family to work in a profession. Like many Welshmen, Albert was very emotional, swinging from extremes of happiness to deep depression. Albert did not figure high in his sons' lives, as he was at the office from early morning to night, handling legal cases. Flora, a native of Northern Ireland, was the daughter of an Anglican minister, descending from a long line of respected lawyers and clergy.

C. S. Lewis was born in Belfast, Ireland, on November 29, 1898. He was baptized Clive Staples Lewis in the staid Church of England of the Victorian era. Collars and backs were stiff. Manners were formal, and little boys were expected to be seen and not heard. However, this would have been difficult in the Lewis household, where Warnie and Jack, with boundless energy, had the run of house and garden. They could shout when excited as well as the next youngster. It was Nurse Endicott's job to keep the boys under control. Their mother ran the household with the assistance of a cook, two parlor maids, and the gardener.

Although other children lived in the neighborhood and the boys had cousins their age nearby, Jack and Warnie found their greatest enjoyment in each other. They played together every day, usually indoors, as Belfast was rainy and foggy.

Mr. Lewis turned out to be very successful in his law firm and decided that his family must have a bigger, more pretentious house. He selected a large site with a view of Belfast's busy harbor and then had a three-story brick Victorian house constructed. He named their new home "Little Lea."

Jack was seven when the family moved to Little Lea. The house had many rooms, long dark halls, and gurgling plumbing. What delighted the boys most were its several attics. These they quickly took over as their private domain. Here they wrote stories and drew pictures, always based on their main interests: talking animals, knights in armor, and the icy northlands. Jack always referred to the two homes he lived in as a child as the "Old House" and the "New House."

Life at Little Lea would have been pure delight for Jack if Warren, by then ten, had not been sent off to boarding school in England. Jack, still without playmates in the neighborhood, had only the servants and his vivid imagination as friends. But once he learned to read, Jack made books his daily companions. Both boys lived their entire lives surrounded by books. At Little Lea, books lay piled two deep in rows of bookcases crowding every room and hall. There were books lying about on tables and chairs, desks, stairwells, and ottomans. Almost every night, Mr. Lewis arrived home with his arms laden with books for Flora, the boys, and himself.

Jack continued to make the attic his favorite spot. There he kept his paints, paper, pen, and ink. Now instead of drawing knights in armor, he began writing and illustrating his first book, *Animal Land*.

No one stopped Jack from reading anything he liked. His parents never said, "You're too young," or "This book is over your head." They allowed him to explore novels, history, poetry, and biographies as he crammed his young head with every kind of literature. But it soon became evident that what Jack enjoyed most was fantasy, particularly the tales of Beatrix

Potter's Peter Rabbit. He searched out the unexpected and the imaginative.

While counting the days until Warnie came home from school on holiday, Jack turned to his mother for companionship. Mother and son took afternoon walks together and trips to the seaside. They even traveled to France to improve Jack's French. Returning by way of London, Jack toured the Tower of London and the zoo. On returning to Belfast, Jack looked forward to seeing his older brother at Christmas. In mid-December Warnie would be arriving home after traveling across the sea from Liverpool. It would be a joyous reunion for both.

At a dormer window in the attic, Jack knelt facing the road winding up from the harbor. Suddenly, a coach came into view. Jack flew down the stairway and out to the white stone steps of the porch.

"Warnie, Warnie!" he shouted as the coach pulled into the circular drive.

Warren leaped out the vehicle's door, not bothering with the steps the coachman pulled down for him. He rushed toward his little brother and, pumping his hand up and down, said, "Oh Jack, it's so great to be home."

Jack looked at Warnie, now taller and older. Warnie was more like a young gentleman than the carefree boy who had left for school at the end of summer.

As the boys entered the front hall, their mother emerged from her sewing room. "Dear boy," she beamed, patting Warnie's shoulder, "How I have missed you!" The pink-cheeked Irish maids in their starched aprons and caps came forward to curtsey. "Welcome home, Master Warren," they chirped.

At six that evening, Mr. Lewis arrived home from his office. Pride showed in his face as he greeted his older son. "Now, Warren," he stated, "I shall expect to see some manly behavior around here for a change."

Jack's heart sank. He knew Father was referring to him. Mr. Lewis, working in the pragmatic field of law, found it disturbing that his younger son took no interest in sports or politics but was rather inclined to keep to himself. Worse yet, Jack was still engrossed within a fantasy world of rabbits, mice, and elves.

Once the greetings were over, Jack dragged Warnie to their favorite spot in the attic.

"Look, Warnie," he cried with delight, "I've been writing a book while you were gone. It's called *Animal Land,* and I'm giving it to Mother for her birthday."

"Let's see," said Warnie, holding out his hand. "Oh, you've even illustrated it. I can't say which I like best, the pictures or the story." Jack relished Warnie's every word.

"There's lots more," added Jack. "I'm even planning a chapter on India—just for you."

Since early childhood, Warnie had been intrigued by that exotic subcontinent, then Britain's wealthiest colony.

"Oh, India," Warnie shrugged his shoulders, "I have other interests now."

Jack looked crestfallen. Had boarding school changed his best and only friend? Jack might even have dropped a tear, except that the dinner bell rang.

"I'd better wash up," Warnie said, appearing more mature by the minute. "See you downstairs."

Jack would have raced to the table with his usual grimy hands, but Miss Harper caught him on the landing. Soon the noisy plumbing rattled loudly, announcing that Jack had obeyed his governess.

Christmas was a delight. Everyone was in the best of moods. Candles flickered on drooping branches of a tall evergreen tree set in a sandbox in the formal living room. Gaslight shed a glow over the stacks of gifts, alluringly waiting to be opened. Each time a guest arrived and the front door opened, the wind blew in stiffly from the sea, trailing a chill into the foyer.

The Lewis household already numbered six: Mr. and Mrs. Lewis; Mr. Lewis's old father, almost blind and very deaf; the boys, Jack and Warnie; and their governess, Miss Harper. Now in quick succession arrived Uncle Joe, Albert Lewis's brother, and Cousin Mary.

There was a marked contrast between Jack's relatives on the Lewis side and the Hamiltons on his mother's. Uncle Joe Lewis had three girls and two boys, one of whom had been a playmate of Jack's in his nursery years. Uncle Joe was fond of Jack. He always treated the boy warmly but seldom entered into conversation with him or his own five children. At Uncle Joe's house, adults spoke rarely to children, engaging them only to ruffle their hair or talk down to them.

Jack found his mother's brother, A. W. Hamilton, more to his liking. "Uncle Gussie" told Jack fascinating stories about science and history and about places he

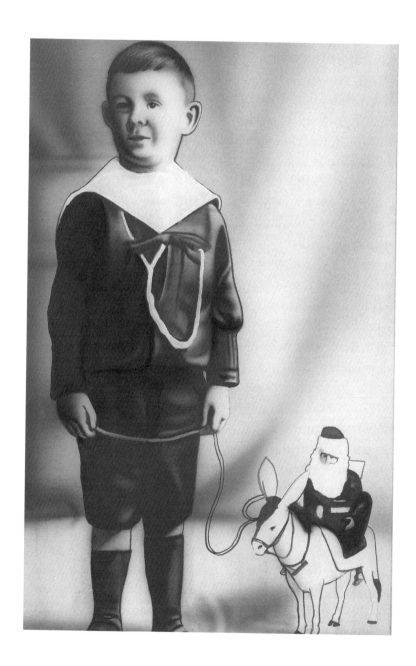

had visited. He opened new horizons to this all-absorbing child, which later enhanced Jack's science fiction and stories about legendary times and people.

As this large, extended family sat before the shining silver and heaped-up plates of their Christmas dinner, Jack felt a surge of joy. Here he found complete happiness: a loving family, fun and laughter, and delightful Christmas delicacies. Added to that was Father's deep voice presenting toasts and sharing jokes and stories.

Jack's father was at his best around a crowded table. He had a great gift for storytelling, and one anecdote followed another, drawing peals of laughter from the diners.

Over the long holiday, Jack and Warnie took walks, rode their bikes, and on snowy days raced down the steep hill to the valley below on their sleds. Jack wondered who needed a close friend or "kissing cousin" with such a wonderful older brother to share his life.

All too soon, Warnie boarded the ship again for Liverpool, off to another term at school, which now owned his allegiance. Somehow, Warnie never mentioned life at boarding school. If Jack questioned him about his studies or friends there, a cloud came over Warnie's jovial face. He seemed reluctant to share anything about his school, all with good reason, as Jack later discovered.

With Warnie gone, Jack found a new love: the long-ago and far-off northlands. He reveled in Nordic mythology, the strong warrior gods, the ice-draped lands of blue and white shadow. He couldn't find enough books and illustrations to satisfy his new hunger. When he asked his father to bring him books on the Norseland, Mr. Lewis appeared distant, as though his mind and heart were in some other far-off place. It wasn't too long before Jack discovered what was troubling his father.

One night Jack lay in bed with a toothache. The pain was caused by a baby tooth, and the family dentist had judged it not worth filling. He knew it would soon fall out anyway. But the boy was also running a fever. He tossed and turned, begging the governess to fetch his mother, but no one seemed interested in his problem.

"Doesn't any one care about me?" he moaned, kicking off the blanket that was quickly drawn up by Miss Parker. "Where's Mummy? Doesn't she know I'm sick?"

Miss Parker put a finger to her lips. "Hush Jack. Your parents can't come right now."

It was then that Jack took notice of the unusual number of people passing up and down the staircase, of the click of unfamiliar shoes on the landing, of strange voices whispering in the hallways. Suddenly Jack's heart went cold.

"Is something wrong?" he asked the stone-faced governess. "Is it Mother?"

Miss Parker's usually stalwart face crumbled. She held a lace-edged handkerchief to her eyes. "Yes, Jack. I'm afraid your mother is quite ill. Several doctors have been with her all evening."

Just then there was a knock at the nursery door. Mr. Lewis entered, looking as if he had been in a battle.

Tears poured down his broad Welsh face. He sat on Jack's bed and took the boy's hot, trembling hand in his.

"Jack," he began, his throat so tight and hoarse that the boy could hardly understand him. "Your mother is very ill. The doctors have been examining her all day. I'm afraid Mother has cancer."

The frightening word *cancer* was then rarely uttered in polite society. Jack pulled the covers over his head and pushed himself down to the bottom of the bed.

"Cancer," he cried. "Cancer means she's going to die."

The little bed shook with his sobs. To the lonely child, Mother meant everything lovely, beautiful, and good. Mother provided stability and understanding, warmth and safety. What would life be without Mother?

The next few months passed in a haze of tragedy. Mrs. Lewis was operated on at home, and the cancer was removed. Everyone in the house looked forward to her fast recovery and a return to normalcy. Brought up in the Church of England, Jack now turned to God, begging him to spare his mother. This was Jack's first great test of faith, but, it seemed, God let him down.

The cancer struck again, this time with greater force as it spread throughout his mother's body.

Warnie returned home for the summer holiday.

"Stop that noise," Jack and his brother were instructed whenever they tried to play. "Go outside. You're disturbing your mother," said the nurses who attended Mrs. Lewis around the clock.

Jack tiptoed into her room for a good-night kiss during a moment when his mother was awake. Doses of morphine had relieved her pain but left her in a twilight condition of sleep. Antiseptic odors, cotton bandages, syringes—all so strange and foreign to Jack's experience—dominated her room. It would be the last time he saw his beloved mother. Returning to his room, Jack heard footsteps padding by his door en route to hers at all hours. His mother's screams of pain pierced the walls near his bed. The terrified boy prayed harder than ever for his mother's life.

Then, on the night of August 23, 1908, Flora Lewis's suffering finally came to an end. Albert visited the nursery to break the news to both boys.

Jack was only nine, his brother thirteen, when their mother died. As the many months of sickness crawled past, Jack had believed that God would spare her. Where was his powerful God, and why had he turned a deafened ear to Jack's desperate prayers? Beyond losing his mother, Jack felt betrayed by God. His faith faltered.

After Flora's death, Albert Lewis seemed to have forgotten his two sons altogether. His heart, his life, was Flora, and she had left him. He had no time for Jack and Warnie, who were suffering as great a loss as he. Deep in grief, Mr. Lewis was completely blinded to anything around him and especially to the needs of his two young sons. But as he grew further apart from them, the two boys grew closer to each other.

Minutes after Flora's death, the somber Irish maids had tiptoed around the house, drawing the heavy drapes and curtains closed. In that moment of sorrow, a dark curtain fell over Jack's childhood. Could anything, or anyone, ever open it again?

CHAPTER TWO

SCHOOL DAYS

Left alone with servants day after day, Jack yearned for time with his brother or father. But totally obsessed with his own grief, Albert Lewis arrived home from the office only to withdraw to his study and his books. He drowned his heartbreak in depression and solitude.

Jack desperately needed the love of a parent, but Albert continued to grieve alone, ignoring the equally great pain of his younger son.

Totally at a loss as to how he might console his son, Albert called Jack to his study.

"Sit down, son," he said. "I have to talk to you."

Jack dropped down to a footstool at his father's feet.

"I realize how much you miss your brother," Albert continued, "and this house is filled with memories of your mother. I don't think it's good for you to be alone here with no one but the servants."

Jack felt an alarm go off. What awful solution had his father come up with? Another wife? A move?

But no. Mr. Lewis continued. "I have made arrangements for you to attend the Wynyard School with Warren."

Jack's face brightened. Nothing gave him greater happiness than being with his older brother. At school they could enjoy activities together again.

Albert's voice droned on behind the curtain of Jack's fantasy. "You will return to Wynyard with Warnie after his next school holiday. I'm sure living together with other boys your own age will help you forget our tragedy."

Jack struck his leg with a clenched fist. "Never, Father! Never! I'll never, *ever* forget Mother." Tears filled the boy's eyes and ran down his round cheeks. He struggled to speak. "May I go now, Father?" he asked, pulling a large white handkerchief from his pocket.

Albert Lewis seemed embarrassed by his son's display of emotion. But hadn't he himself also paced and wept almost constantly over the past few months? Theirs was a home broken by tragedy, overshadowed by ghosts of happier times.

Leaving his father's study, Jack turned to say, "You're right. Maybe things will be better far away from here. At least I'll be with Warnie." Then Jack quietly closed the door to leave his grieving father with his thoughts. It seemed to Jack that he had not only lost his mother but was now about to lose his father as well. His only joy was the prospect of joining Warnie for a new life at a new school.

But nothing would prove easy for Jack at his new boarding school. Home on holidays, Warnie had been tight-lipped about the realities of Wynyard and its sadistic schoolmaster. Young Jack left home blissfully unaware of what lay ahead.

British middle- and upper-class boys are generally sent away at age eight to prep schools. These smaller boarding schools prepare youngsters for entrance into upper grades at expensive private schools, such as Eton and Harrow, where Greek, Latin, and the classics are taught. These schools turn out "proper English gentlemen," ready, hopefully, to enter Oxford or Cambridge.

But Wynyard was a prep school where morale and education were at their lowest. What made Albert select such a school for his motherless boys? Albert Lewis had written his former headmaster, W. T. Kirkpatrick, for advice. After receiving a suggested list from Kirkpatrick, Albert wrote the recommended schools for information but never took the time to visit even one of them.

Also, Albert Lewis suffered from a constant fear of financial ruin and took care to spend the least amount of money possible. Consequently, he selected the school with the lowest tuition. It came at a great cost to his sons.

In September 1908, nine-year-old Jack left home to begin his new life at Wynyard. Mr. Lewis hired a carriage to take the three of them to the docks of Belfast.

There awaited a small steamer on which the boys would sail to Liverpool.

The boys were dressed in formal dark suits, high Eton collars, and tight bowler hats. They looked forlorn and depressed as the horses pulled them through the cobblestone streets from Little Lea to the piers and ships on the lough.

At that time, Belfast was a thriving port city of 350,000 people, mostly English families with a Church of England background. There were also many Scotch Presbyterians. The small Catholic colony was made up of dock workers and parlor maids.

Belfast's main source of wealth was shipbuilding, plus the manufacturing of linen cloth. Freighters, tall-masted sailing ships, and British naval vessels filled the busy harbor.

Jack gazed back longingly at Belfast's green hills and his home—the one place he had always felt safe and secure. What awaited him in England? What would the school be like? How strange that Warnie had never shared his experiences at Wynyard with Jack or his father. Was it a point of pride, an expression of Warnie's growing maturity now that he was thirteen?

Mr. Lewis left the boys, saying good-bye once they were settled in their tiny cabin. After they left the harbor, Jack became thrilled with his first sea voyage: the working of the ship and the harbor lights and rolling waves. The rough Irish seas had the opposite effect on Warnie, who spent most of the night wretched with nausea.

Early the next morning, the ship docked in Liverpool, where the brothers boarded a train to Euston. Jack was disappointed by the flat, ugly landscape, as well as by the unfamiliar English accents all around him. His ears were accustomed to the soft Irish lilt of his homeland.

The reality of Wynyard came as a total shock. The school was located in a small semiattached house made of yellow brick. The eight boarders slept on narrow metal cots in an attic dormitory. The toilets were outhouses in an iron shed. The boys were allowed only one bath a week. As an adult, Jack would refer to the school as "Belsen," in reference to the infamous Nazi prison camp.

The school's only teacher was the headmaster, the Reverend Robert Capron, a clergyman of the Church of England. He ruled the students and his family with a heavy hand. On the classroom stove hung a thick brown cane, which he used to teach as well as to discipline. Capron, nicknamed "Oldie," would select certain boys, usually those on scholarship, as his victims. Neither Lewis boy ever felt his sadistic arm, and Jack, still a little fellow with a chubby, round face, was fortunate to become the cruel clergyman's pet.

Wynyard had none of the traditional playing fields where happy boys in white outfits played cricket or soccer. The only recreation available was an afternoon walk on sunny days.

Long ago, Oldie was said to have imbued his students with a love of knowledge, but, by 1908, his one remaining talent seemed to be the teaching of geometry. Otherwise, the boys learned nothing.

Mealtimes were like scenes from *Oliver Twist*. Fear knotted Jack's stomach at every meal as each day's unidentifiable slop was placed before him. Who would be thrashed? Which student humiliated? Any boy who left something on his plate was cruelly punished. There was no one to offer support and nowhere to go to escape the tyranny. Capron's timid wife and somberly dressed daughters were no help. They never spoke but, on being questioned by their father, whispered humbly, "Yes, Father. No, Father."

Capron's son, Wynyard, who had been mercilessly flogged by his father throughout his schooldays, was a broken man. He lived at the school and helped with the boys.

Jack repeatedly wrote his father, pleading to come home. Jack's gentle, romantic nature quailed at the suffering he witnessed every day at Wynyard. In addition, he had learned absolutely nothing while there.

Warnie suggested to his father that he and Jack would be better off attending Campbell College, only blocks from their home in Belfast.

Finally, Albert Lewis relented and enrolled Warnie at Campbell. But poor Jack was forced to remain at Wynyard for another two terms. By then the school was down to only five boarders, and Oldie decided to close his school permanently. Not long after, he was judged insane and spent the rest of his life in a mental institution. Mr. Lewis had done poorly in selecting a school for his boys. Jack was scarred for life by the experience. When Belsen closed, Mr. Lewis finally enrolled Jack at Campbell in Belfast.

By then Jack was eager to learn and found life at Campbell happy and stimulating. It was there that he first fell in love with poetry, on hearing his teacher read Matthew Arnold's *Sohrab and Rustum*.

One Friday, Jack came home from school with a deep, rattling cough. For once, his father showed concern for the boy. He decided Jack needed a climate dryer than the damp mists of Belfast. Warnie was now off attending school in Malvern, England, a town renowned as a health resort for people with lung diseases. Albert was quick to admit that Jack had a "poor chest," the poorest he had ever seen in a boy of Jack's age. Something had to be done.

So after but one term at the Belfast school, Jack was shipped to Cherbourg, a small prep school also located in Malvern. Since Warnie attended Malvern College in the same city, the brothers could travel there together. At Malvern green hills surrounded the white, regency-style school that Jack attended, and the food and education there were far superior to that of Wynyard.

Jack liked the school as well as the town. He was popular with the students because of his humor and storytelling ability, though on the playing fields he was thwarted by his unbendable thumbs, baby fat, and weak muscles.

There were several excellent teachers for the seventeen boys who made up Jack's class. The faculty was able to help Jack catch up in the courses he needed in order to win a scholarship to Malvern College. Jack excelled in Latin and English and quickly made up for the two years wasted at Wynyard. Poetry fired his romantic imagination. Jack began reading books way beyond his years.

But it was during this period that C. S. Lewis, later to become the great apologist for Christianity, cast off the faith of his forefathers and the Church of England. He became an atheist, no longer believing in God or in his son, Jesus Christ.

As the boys at Cherbourg were all quite young, the school employed a matron who cared for the youngsters in place of a mother. Miss Cowie nursed the boys when they were sick, bandaged the wounds they received on the playing fields, and offered them consolation when they needed it.

Unfortunately, Miss Cowie also shared with Jack a strange new interest—a fascination with the occult. Jack had always been drawn to the unseen world of fairies, goblins, and little people. Now he began secretly to substitute Miss Cowie's beliefs in spiritualism, theosophy, and other aspects of the occult for his earlier Christian beliefs. The matron gradually drew Jack away from his nightly prayers. A lonely boy, left motherless, Jack found everything he needed in her newfound attention and direction.

One night the headmaster discovered Miss Cowie holding the now thirteen-year-old Jack in her arms. Suspected of leading the boy astray, she was fired on the spot. With the matron gone, Jack centered his attention on a young teacher nicknamed "Pogo" by the students. Having already abandoned his faith, which had kept him on the "straight and narrow," Jack now began to copy the worldly ways of his new idol. Pogo opened Jack's eyes to all that was fashionable. Jack began to dress stylishly and affected Pogo's swagger and snobbish mannerisms. Jack seemed to have been transformed into another person. Warnie had already gone that route and saw nothing unusual about the change in his brother, now flashy and almost vulgar. But one aspect of this was to the good.

At Cherbourg, Jack was first introduced to culture and the arts. He attended performances of Shakespearean plays, Handel's *Messiah*, and the operas of Richard Wagner, which became a lifelong love. Wagner's music also contributed to Jack's growing interest in everything Teutonic: northern, cold, pale, and remote. Jack bought recordings of Wagnerian operas and listened to them with relish on his windup Victrola.

The high quality of education at Cherbourg and Jack's great interest in the classics led to his applying for a scholarship to Malvern College. Almost prophetically, one of the examining teachers wrote of Jack's work, "I believe he is just the sort we should develop to take a classics award at Oxford."

Warnie, on the other hand, had done so poorly at Malvern that he was asked to leave. However, after some tutoring by Mr. Lewis's former headmaster, W. T.

Kirkpatrick, Warnie was accepted at Sandhurst, Britain's foremost military academy, where he went on to prepare for a military career. At least Albert Lewis could take pride in his younger son's scholastic success, for Jack did win the coveted scholarship and admission to Malvern.

Jack entered Malvern College, the equivalent of an American prep school, in the fall term of 1913. He was fourteen: tall, awkward, and totally nonathletic.

As a new and junior boy at Malvern, Jack was expected to polish the seniors' shoes, run their errands, and take endless abuse from them. This was called "faggin'." Jack resented it. He had expected the older boys, who had attended classes with his brother, to include him in their circles. But as a soft-faced new boy, he was quite beneath their notice.

Jack's introduction to Malvern proved unexpectedly blunt and cruel. Malvern had five hundred students who were quartered in several large buildings or "houses."

With his brother now gone off to be a cadet at Sandhurst, young Jack was left with no one to show him around and explain the rules and traditions of the school.

On his second day at Malvern, he approached an older boy, a prefect, and asked for help.

"Excuse me, sir," said the innocent new student. "How can I find out which club I've been assigned to?"

"Oh, I say, Lewis," the tall senior bawled out, "you are in the same club as I am. It's B6."

Almost floating above the floor at being addressed by someone of such importance, Jack thanked him profusely and went to find it.

For a full week, Jack reported each afternoon to B6, searching to see if his name had been posted there for some required sport. It never was. In a secret way, Jack felt relieved: He accepted sports as one of the necessary evils of life. But then the axe fell. The senior boy had lied to him! Actually, Jack had been assigned to a totally different club. His name had appeared on the list several days during which he had not shown up. At Malvern this was a serious offense. The punishment was a flogging to be administered by "Porridge," the head student, in front of the college president.

A pimply boy soon summoned Jack to the flogging. Adding insult to injury, the boy sneered at Jack as they walked to the president's office.

"Who are you?" the boy asked.

"Nobody!" responded Jack, adding, "Who is Porridge?"

"Why, the most important person there is!" declared the escort.

From this painful beating, C. S. Lewis learned an important lesson: Never rely on secondhand information.

Warnie had loved Malvern but didn't do well there. Jack was a top student and hated it. Boys at Malvern were much more interested in sports than in scholarship. They also used the school for their social advancement. Jack despised both sports and social climbing.

Tired out by the heavy burden of homework, added to the time spent "faggin'," Jack never had a free moment. He soon fell ill with bronchitis and spent two weeks in the school's infirmary. Upon recovering, he wrote his father several times, begging to be allowed to come home. "I'm unhappy and exhausted," he declared. Finally, when Jack threatened to kill himself, Albert Lewis became sufficiently alarmed to take action.

Once again, Mr. Lewis wrote to his old schoolmaster, W. T. Kirkpatrick, asking for help in making arrangements for Jack to study privately and to complete his schooling under the teacher's direction.

On arriving home in Belfast, Jack learned that soon he'd be going back to England, this time to live with Kirkpatrick and his wife in the village of Great Bookham, Surrey. There would be no other boys, no faggin', no sports, his father assured him. Better yet, Mrs. Kirkpatrick, a plump, shallow woman, was an excellent cook. After Jack's years of wretched boarding-school meals, he looked forward to this with delight. Jack would soon devour everything she prepared.

As for Mr. Kirkpatrick—tall, thin, bald, with bushy sideburns—he was like no other schoolmaster Jack had ever known. Kirkpatrick was determined to bring out the best in his new student. He questioned Jack's every statement. "Do you have proof?" he would ask. "Is that really what you mean?" Beyond this, Kirkpatrick, himself an ardent atheist, put a sharp edge on Lewis's now complete embrace of atheism.

Kirkpatrick assigned books and then questioned Jack like a lawyer cross-examining a witness about everything in each work. But Jack liked nothing better than reading. He studied all of the greatest classics, often in the original Greek and Latin, and committed many to memory.

After a morning of intense work, Jack and Kirkpatrick would set out on foot across the countryside, still discussing what Jack had read and studied. It was a delightful and unusual way to learn, and Jack reveled in it.

It was during this period that the First World War broke out. Warnie was immediately called up for service and sent to the western front. During that summer break, alone at home with his father in Belfast, Jack discovered a new and wonderful companion—Arthur Greeves. Arthur had attended Campbell College with Jack, but since they were three years apart in age, it at first seemed they had nothing in common.

Arthur lived not far from the Lewis home, Little Lea. That summer Jack received a letter from Arthur stating that he was ill in bed and would enjoy a visit from Jack. Jack hardly remembered the older boy but felt obliged to respond.

When he entered the sickroom, Jack discovered a young man with beautiful features: golden hair and blue eyes. Pale and listless, Arthur was propped up in bed on a pile of pillows. What caught Jack's eye, however, was an open book at Arthur's bedside entitled *Myths of the Norsemen*.

"Do you like this book?" asked Jack, fingering it lovingly.

"Do you like it?" asked Arthur with mounting excitement. Jack could hardly believe his good fortune. Here was another young man who loved stories of the north as much as he did. Both grabbed at the book, talking, pointing, quoting, almost shouting—reveling in their surprising discovery. They loved the same tales, even the same parts of the book. In that moment, Jack found a lifelong friend. Here, at last, was someone with whom he could share his greatest interest, his innermost thoughts. Lonely young Jack had discovered someone much like himself.

The next two years were spent studying privately under the tutelage of Mr. Kirkpatrick. In his free time, Jack wrote poems and essays. Able to advance at his own pace, Jack covered all the material required for the entrance exams at Oxford and expanded his knowledge and creativity at an amazing speed. Kirkpatrick wrote to Albert Lewis, "Jack has read more classics than anyone I know, unless it be Addison or Macauley." Not long after, on December 14, 1916, Jack learned that he had won the coveted Classic Scholarship at University College. He had just turned eighteen.

CHAPTER THREE

WAR AND PEACE

Lewis, now a young gentleman of eighteen, spent the summer break back at Little Lea, getting to know his father as a friend for the first time. Then Jack was soon reading for his first term at Oxford. He had not been accepted at Keble College, the college of his choice, because he was very poor at mathematics and had no knowledge of any branch of science. He was, however, a brilliant classical scholar, having read all of the Greek poets in their original language. These accomplishments met the requirements of University College, where he was accepted.

In 1917, upon arriving at Oxford, C. S. Lewis moved into his quarters at University College to start the fall term. Oxford was a medieval city of beauty and charm. Tall spires and towers of chapels and churches reached into the sky. The ancient streets wound around and across the Rivers Isis and Cherwell, where students punted small wooden boats or raced long sculls.

Each college surrounded a large courtyard; its single entrance passed through a guarded gatehouse or "porter's lodge," which opened onto a small enclosed world of classrooms and living quarters with a large dining hall and chapel. Every student was required to take part in chapel services.

At this point in his life, Lewis was an avowed atheist. He despised having to attend the Anglican services, although later in life he would be glad to have been exposed to the beautiful phrasing of the Book of Common Prayer and the King James Bible.

University College was in the heart of Oxford. The city was quaint, with old pubs, exquisite architecture, and formal gardens; Lewis fell in love with it. Little did he know that he would spend the rest of his life there.

As winner of a coveted scholarship, Lewis was entitled to quarters within the college. They consisted of the traditional two rooms: one for sleeping, the other for studying. The study was a large, nicely furnished room with a fireplace. A servant (called a "scout") brought hot water each morning for Lewis to shave with. The scout also provided tea and cleaned the rooms. Jack was able to devote all his time to study and reading. His only recreation was walking in the countryside and swimming in the nearby river.

Jack had been at Oxford only a short time when he realized that, as a university student in England, he faced the prospect of being drafted into the British army. World War I was raging on the continent. As did many of his fellow students, Jack chose to enlist in the

University Officers Training Corps rather than wait to be drafted. Fortunately, his early training was in a company billeted at Oxford's Keble College. After only a month, he was commissioned as a second lieutenant in the Somerset Light Infantry.

While training at Keble, Lewis shared a room with a young man named Edward Francis Moore, nicknamed "Paddy" for his Irish background. The two became fast friends. Before leaving for the front, Jack and Paddy had a serious conversation about their respective futures. In their small uncarpeted room, Jack sat on his narrow bed and looked deep into his friend's eyes.

"You know, Paddy, if we are sent to the front, there's a good chance one of us may get killed."

Paddy stood up and paced the tiny room.

"Yes, I know. And it makes me worry about my mother and sister. Who will look after them? Maureen is only a child, and Mum is raising her alone. I'd love for you to meet them. They are staying in Bristol while I'm here in training."

Jack put away the book he had planned to read that evening.

"Paddy," he sighed on the brink of tears. "You needn't worry. I promise to look after them—whatever happens over there."

"And I swear I'll look after your father—if anything happens to you."

The young men solemnly shook hands on the promise. Who could have suspected that promise would affect Lewis for the next thirty years?

With both Warnie and Jack serving in the British army, their father Albert Lewis was undoubtedly worried. Casualties on both sides of the war were high. Yet, when Jack asked his father to visit him before he left for France, Mr. Lewis replied that he was too busy with his law practice. Always expecting another opportunity, he never went.

Jack was deeply hurt. Other parents were desperate to see their sons one last time before they left for France. Some even moved to Oxford to be near them during training, which is what Paddy's mother had done. Then only forty-five, slim and pretty, Janie Moore had taken rooms outside Oxford with her eleven-year-old daughter, Maureen. Mrs. Moore loved to entertain and opened her furnished rooms to Paddy and his friends. Jack was very taken by the lovely Irish woman and assured her that he would look after Paddy while in France.

"Don't you worry, either," he added. "I'll make sure you and Maureen are always cared for."

Mrs. Moore grabbed his hands and whispered, "You are a fine boy, Jack. I believe you."

On November 15, Jack sent a telegram to his father informing him of another leave. He asked his father one last time to visit him.

Albert Lewis had not read between the lines. Jack meant to convey that this was his final leave before going overseas. Mr. Lewis replied, "Don't understand telegram. Please write." By the time Mr. Lewis had received further explanation, Jack was gone. The young man was deeply hurt and disappointed.

C. S. Lewis

Young Lieutenant Lewis, freshly commissioned, quickly found himself at the front. He arrived at the trenches on the battlefield of the Somme Valley in France on his nineteenth birthday, November 29, 1917. World War I would end just a year later, but not in time to spare Lewis from injury or the painful loss of a dear friend.

Overhead, shells whistled, and the ground shook with the booming of giant cannon, but Jack thought of it at first as a great adventure. He enjoyed fellowship with the other officers in their underground bunkers. He had time to write letters to his father, Arthur, and Mrs. Moore, to whom he was very attracted. Lacking a mother, Jack had welcomed her sympathy and warmth toward him. She affectionately addressed him as "Boysie."

Jack spent much of that winter in the trenches. The trenches were too cold; yet their underground bunker was too hot. The misery was unrelenting. "The winter weariness and water were our chief enemies," he wrote. He walked in the trenches in thigh-high boots with icy water up to his knees. Sometimes, it spilled into his boots, freezing his feet. Meanwhile, the Germans kept up a steady barrage of shells—three a minute, both day and night. Bullets whined right past Jack's head.

Most frightful were the foul odors of the horribly wounded men, of the corpses lying across no-man's-land, with others rotting on the barbed wire.

Jack came down with trench fever, an illness transmitted by body lice. Albert Lewis heard from the war office—"Your son is in the hospital at Le Treport, France." Jack saw it as a chance to rest in a clean dry bed and read.

After spending twenty-seven days in the hospital, Jack was sent back to the front. Nine days later, not long after taking sixty German soldiers prisoner, he was struck by a shell that burst near him. He received three serious wounds from pieces of shrapnel. One piece was lodged near his heart, one injured his left hand, and another entered his leg. The young lieutenant was carried from the front lines by stretcher, ending up in another hospital in France, in Etaples. At almost the same time, Jack's closest friend, Paddy Moore, was killed in battle. Mrs. Moore didn't learn of Paddy's death for over a month.

When Warnie learned of his brother's injuries, he borrowed a bicycle and pedaled from his own army unit in France fifty miles to Etaples to see him. Warnie became very upset at finding his young brother in pain. This reunion healed the coldness that had come between them over the past few years. From this point on, they resumed their close boyhood friendship and would maintain it for the rest of their lives.

Jack wrote home from the French hospital on both May 4 and June 14, giving his father details of his injuries. Next, he was transferred to a hospital in London. Lonely and depressed, he telegraphed his father, begging him to visit. On June 20 Jack wrote again, "You will be able to come over, if only for a few days."

But Albert never came. He begged off, writing that he had bronchitis and couldn't travel. However, Mr. Lewis never missed a single day at the office!

Jack wrote that he would soon be transferred to a convalescent home. He added, "Wherever I am, I know that you will come and see me." The lonely patient, still in great pain, endured the added suffering caused by his father, who never took the time to visit.

But Mrs. Moore did. She came to the London hospital several times. Horribly homesick, Jack asked to be transferred to a convalescent home near his father. Unable to do so, he chose instead one in Bristol, close to where Mrs. Moore was then living. On June 24 Jack was sent to the nursing home in Bristol for two months of convalescence. It was a thirteenth-century castle set in a deer park. As Jack regained strength, he walked about the grounds, often coming upon a startled stag.

Mrs. Moore, not surprisingly, needed comfort and affection as much as Jack did. Her only son, Paddy, had been killed on the battlefield. Jack was very mindful of his promise to Paddy and Mrs. Moore. So was she.

Janie Moore came regularly to see Jack at the home, and, as soon as he was well enough, she invited him to stay with her and her daughter Maureen in Bristol. There Mrs. Moore dispensed warmth and hospitality, along with home-cooked meals and delicacies. Of Paddy's many friends, all but Jack had died in the Battle of the Somme. She wrote to Jack's father, "I feel I can never do enough for those boys who are left. Jack has been so good to me. My poor son asked him to look after me if he did not come back. For a boy his age, Jack possesses such a wonderful power of understanding and sympathy."

Jack had already taken Mrs. Moore on as a second mother. He felt great pity for her as she grieved the loss of her only son, whereas Jack's own father had let him down throughout the months of his convalescence. Is it any wonder that the wounded youth now focused all his affection on Mrs. Moore. He soon came to call her "Mother" or "Minto."

Finally the war ended. Church bells pealed; fireworks lit the skies; people danced in the streets. As soon as Jack was fully recovered, he looked forward to returning to Oxford for the spring term. Meanwhile, he was free to return to Belfast for Christmas, where father and son used the opportunity to seek a resolution to their hurt.

It was also a time of joy and pride. Jack had compiled a collection of poems he'd written between the ages of fifteen and nineteen. A London publisher had accepted the small manuscript, entitled *Spirits in Bondage*. C. S. Lewis's first book received excellent reviews in the *London Times* and other papers. His writing career had begun.

Jack was thrilled to be at Oxford once more. Nothing had changed, except now there were twenty-eight students at University College, all of them mature after their war experiences. The large dining hall was reopened, and breakfast was no longer served in the scholars' rooms.

Although Jack had not completed the math require-
ment for entry to Oxford, men who had served in the
war were released from taking the exam. This was fortunate, as Jack had not been able to pass the required
math test the first time.

For the injuries he received in the war, Lewis was
given a small pension. This helped pay for his first two
years at college. His father also contributed toward
Jack's support and was delighted at Jack's being a published author.

Lewis threw himself into his studies. However, he
always found time to write to his friend in Belfast,
Arthur Greeves. Jack treasured every letter that came
from Arthur and was frank and open in his correspondence. But to his father, he wrote only of practi-
cal matters. While they had reconciled to a degree, a
true bridge of friendship seemed impossible between
father and son. Meanwhile, Jack's friendship with Mrs.
Moore deepened daily. Jack took the place of the son
she had lost in the war, and she, in turn, took the place
of the mother Jack had lost to cancer.

Janie Moore had been separated from her husband
for years. She had no means of support other than
what Mr. Moore sent for their daughter Maureen's
care. Often, the money was delayed or never arrived.
Sensing it was his duty, due to his promise to Paddy,
Jack often contributed small amounts to tide them
over.

During a visit of Jack's to Belfast, Albert Lewis discovered that his son's bank account was overdrawn. He

was furious to learn that the money he had sent Jack for college was instead going to support Mrs. Moore. Albert was totally puzzled by his son's involvement with a woman twenty-four years his senior.

Jack began winning important awards in three areas of study: Greek and Latin literature in 1920, philosophy and ancient history in 1922, and English in 1923. Each of these exams lasted six days. It was a great honor for one so young to win the top grades. He also won the Chancellor's Prize for the finest essay written by an Oxford undergraduate in 1923 and was appointed a tutor at University College following graduation. On May 20, 1924, Lewis was elected a fellow of Magdalen College. He gladly accepted.

With this position, Lewis received a suite of rooms in the college, a salary, and an elevated seat at the dons' "high table" in the dining hall. His primary duty was to tutor individual students at Magdalen College in English language and literature. He began his life as an Oxford don in 1925. He would continue in that position for the next twenty-nine years.

Meanwhile, Mrs. Moore rented a house in nearby Headington Quarry. Maureen and Jack joined her there. Jack made the care of his friend's mother and sister a lifetime priority.

Jack's brother, now Major Warren Lewis, remained in the military, stationed at various posts around the world. When home on leave, Warnie was intensely jealous of the time his brother spent with Janie Moore. So, too, was Albert Lewis. Both were deeply concerned about Jack's growing emotional attachment to Mrs. Moore. Although no longer a churchgoer, Lewis was always highly moral in all aspects of his life.

Throughout his years of study at Oxford, Lewis remained a very convinced atheist. He had abandoned his Christian faith as an adolescent and stayed away from the church well into adulthood. Neither the stress of battle, the pain of his wounds, nor his separation from loved ones had turned his heart toward God.

But, as in "The Hound of Heaven," the poem by Francis Thompson, God eventually tracked Lewis down: not through sermons or a blinding vision, but by way of books and friends, which Jack loved most.

CHAPTER FOUR

CONVERSION

C. S. Lewis, the pragmatic atheist and lover of fantasy, did not experience a sudden conversion. His transformation into a Christian developed over a period of years.

The Anglican services he attended as a child in Belfast were presided over by his maternal grandfather. Both Jack and Warnie were bored and put off by the studied ritual and their grandfather's emotional sermons.

Many times Jack searched for something he called "the supreme spirit" through a personal form of meditation. He sought to quiet the constant motion of thoughts passing through his mind so he could be in the presence of pure spirit. On the other hand, he dabbled in mystics, Freudian psychology, and a great deal more. It became increasingly clear to this brilliant seeker that he was in an unholy muddle. What, or who, could clear it up?

The seeds for his eventual conversion had been planted earlier in his teens through his reading of George MacDonald's *Phantastes*. Jack later recorded in his spiritual autobiography, *Surprised by Joy,* that it was through *Phantastes* that he first experienced holiness and the holy and that his imagination was truly baptized. Much later, after reading *The Everlasting Man,* by G. K. Chesterton, Lewis admitted to himself that "Christianity was very sensible, apart from its Christianity."

God, it seemed, would resort to anything, even using a foe of the faith, to get Jack's attention. Harry Weldon was a fellow tutor at Magdalen College. He was also a cynic who made fun of every religion and all creeds. But it was he, of all people, who stopped Lewis in his tracks.

One cold evening, Harry was smoking before a crackling fire in Lewis's room. Out of the blue, he unexpectedly broached an almost taboo subject. "Actually," he began, "there's plenty of evidence to support the facts of the Gospels."

Lewis looked at Harry as though he had lost his mind. "You've had too much to drink," laughed Jack, knocking the ashes from his pipe.

"No," replied Weldon, "that stuff of Fraser's about the Dying God, it looks as if it really happened once."

Jack refilled his pipe and mulled over his friend's words.

"The Dying God? Why that's Jesus, of course," he thought.

After Harry left, Lewis could not get those words out of his mind. A door had cracked open in the room he had shut off so long ago. Lewis reread the Gospels.

From this time forward, he felt a strong pressure to believe. This was strengthened by two other close friends, Hugo Dyson and J. R. R. Tolkien. Tolkien, later the best-selling author of *The Hobbit* and *The Lord of the Rings,* was a devout Roman Catholic. Both were members of the "Inklings," a group of literary friends Lewis had formed.

Lewis had invited both men as dinner guests in the Great Hall of Magdalen College. Later they strolled around nearby Addison's Walk, talking about myths—a subject of intense interest to all three men. Jack said he loved reading myths but never regarded them as true.

Tolkien shocked the unbeliever by stating, "Myths originate in God and preserve something of God's truth, although often in a distorted form." As Tolkien continued his exposition on myths, a cold wind brushed the trees along Addison's Walk. Lewis took this as a message from God. A chill ran down his spine.

Tolkien continued, "The Christian story is a myth invented by God, whose dying could transform those who believed in him. Jack," added Tolkien, "you must plunge in and hope to find the relevance of God's story to your life."

Lewis was astounded. All his life he had been entranced by myths of all cultures. He had written poems and stories in myth form. But God?

The men continued talking in Lewis's rooms until three in the morning, when Tolkien finally left to go home. But Dyson remained, chatting with Lewis until dawn.

"You see," argued Dyson, "Christianity only works for the believer. He is put at peace and freed from his sins. He can become a new person."

Notwithstanding that Lewis was now surrounded by Christian friends, all of them as brilliant and well read as he, the stubborn atheist still refused to believe.

Then God took over. Lewis described the moment: "Even though the 'Spirit' I was finally accepting differed in some way from the God of popular religion, He [God] would not argue about it. He only said, 'I am The Lord.' 'I am That I am.'"

God demanded a leap in the dark. Each night alone in his room, Lewis felt God approaching closer and closer. Later he wrote, "That which I most feared had at last come upon me in the Trinity Term of 1929. I gave in and admitted that God was God. I knelt and prayed that night, the most reluctant convert in all England."

That first conversion was solely to the one God. Lewis still rejected the concept of God becoming man in the person of Jesus Christ. And yet there was one distinct change in his lifestyle—Lewis began attending church each Sunday, as well as the daily chapel services of Magdalen College. Why such a drastic move when he had not yet accepted the Trinity? In his own words, he declared, "I thought one ought to fly one's flag by some unmistakable outward sign." This was in spite of Lewis's dislike of both hymns and pipe organs.

He was put off even more by the fussy time-wasting of congregational affairs: programs, notices, and meetings. But if he was to obey God, then part of his allegiance must be to worship him in his church, notably his local parish in the established Church of England.

During this entire period, which stretched from Lewis's twenty-ninth to his thirty-first year, Jack had become a close part of the Moore family, moving eleven times as Mrs. Moore's finances fluctuated up and down. Suddenly, he was summoned back to Belfast. Albert Lewis had undergone an operation, during which the surgeon discovered cancer. Father and son had become somewhat reconciled before this, and Jack had visited his father during most holiday vacations. He now tried to make his father as comfortable as possible—feeding him, shaving him, and reading to him.

Upon Albert's apparent recovery from the operation, Jack felt free to return to his teaching. But he was back in Oxford only a few days when a telegram arrived announcing Albert's death on September 24, 1930.

On September 26, Jack wired the sad news to Warnie, who had been stationed with the British army in Shanghai, China, for the past two years. With Warnie on the other side of the world, it fell to Jack to settle his father's affairs, selling Little Lea and disposing of the contents. Mrs. Moore came to Belfast and helped out with decisions on what to leave and what to bring back to Oxford.

Major Lewis's trip back home took a long time. He traveled from Hong Kong by freighter to Japan and then on to San Francisco, then across the United States by train, and across the Atlantic by steamer. While in Shanghai, Warnie had experienced a conversion similar to Jack's. He also returned to the church of his youth. Following Warnie's return to Oxford in 1931, the Lewis brothers thereafter regularly attended services together. But Jack still had reservations about the place of Jesus and the truth of Christian doctrine.

To get around the English countryside, Warnie bought a motorcycle, adding a sidecar for a passenger. One clear, sunny morning, on September 22, 1931, he came by Magdalen College. Revving his bike, Warnie called out, "Come on, Jack! This is a perfect day to visit the zoo at Whipsnade. Hop in and let's get on our way."

"Just a second, Warnie, let me get my cap, it's rather breezy today."

Jack raced off for his cap and, on his return, climbed into the sidecar. The brothers took off for the zoo. Warnie puttered along, winding though the ancient brick streets of Oxford. Once on London Road, Warnie applied the gas and, with Jack clutching his cap, they sped off toward Whipsnade, just north of London.

Later Jack reported an amazing occurrence. "When we set out, I did not believe that Jesus Christ was the Son of God, and when we reached the zoo, I did!" Without thought, discussion, or emotion, C. S. Lewis had finally stepped over the threshold and was soon to become one of the greatest Christian apologists of our time.

Jack's first effort to describe his conversion in a book was unsatisfactory. He disposed of it and tried another tack, choosing the form of an allegory. He called it *The Pilgrim's Regress,* a play on John Bunyan's *Pilgrim's Progress.* The book was a modest success but disturbed his fellow Oxonians, who considered this public display of religion unmannerly. Some Oxford dons turned their backs on Lewis.

But once Jack had taken a stand for God, such attacks made no dent in his armor. And he had the full support of his brother, now also a practicing Christian.

In 1931 Mrs. Moore received a small inheritance. By then, Albert Lewis's estate had also been settled and was found to be much smaller than Jack and Warren had anticipated. By pooling their assets, however, Warren, Jack, and Mrs. Moore had enough money to invest in a property. They began looking around for a secluded country place that could hold them all, including Maureen, Mrs. Moore's daughter and Paddy's sister. That July they came upon The Kilns, a two-story brick house on eight acres, offered at 3,300 pounds sterling.

This tiny estate was located in Headington Quarry, three miles from Oxford. Holy Trinity, a charming Anglican church, was within walking distance. The estate was called The Kilns because it had once housed the manager of the local brickyard. Two large beehive kilns still hovered like giants behind charming but rather rundown house. The extensive grounds included a large pond stocked with fish, which was also used for swimming, boating, and ice skating. In addition, there were a tennis court, greenhouse, garage, and two small cottages.

Jack and Warnie put up fifteen hundred pounds between them, and Mrs. Moore put up the remaining eighteen hundred pounds. That settled, Janie Moore, her daughter, Maureen, and Jack and Warren Lewis moved into The Kilns. Papers were drawn up listing Mrs. Moore as the sole owner of The Kilns but permitting both brothers to live there until their deaths, at which time the property would become Maureen's.

Also part of the household was Fred Paxford, gardener and handyman, who lived in one of the two cottages. Paxford did the daily shopping and drove the Lewis car, as Jack never learned to drive. In addition, there were usually one or two maids who cleaned and served the meals.

Mrs. Moore ran the household with an iron hand, ordering even the two bachelors to do their part. No sooner had they moved in when all began working to improve the neglected property. Paxford laid walks and had the pond deepened and cleared. Jack enjoyed planting and tending the vegetable garden. He also delighted in walking about the extensive woodlands and taking daily swims in the pond.

Though there were few modern conveniences at The Kilns, the new owners loved its seclusion and beauty. Initially, The Kilns had three modest bedrooms on the second floor. Maureen used the room to the right of the stairs until her marriage in 1940. Mrs. Moore slept in the room immediately to the left. Jack had to pass through Mrs. Moore's room to get to his own, preventing privacy for either of them. He had an outside staircase built to provide direct access to his bedroom so that he need not walk through Mrs. Moore's, either disturbing her or inviting her wrath. At the earliest opportunity, they added a single-story wing on the north side of the house, providing a proper bedroom for Mrs. Moore and releasing her former bedroom to become Jack's study. It was here that he wrote *Chronicles of Narnia.* Later, a bedroom and study would be added to the north wing for Warnie when he retired from the army.

Ancient plumbing in the sole bathroom, located on the first floor, made infernal clanking and whining noises when used. The sounds seemed particularly loud and frightening at night. To save money, the hot water heater was rarely lit, so Jack grew accustomed to washing in cold water in his room. He rarely took a hot bath, even when visiting the homes of friends. He was renowned for his careless appearance and shabby clothing.

In 1931 Major Lewis, still in the service, was ordered to return to Shanghai, where he had charge of the Royal Army Service Corps. Before his departure, the Lewis brothers took the first of many long walking tours in Wales, this one from Chepstow to the ruins of Tintern Abbey. Major Lewis retired from the British army in 1932 and lived on a pension at The Kilns for the rest of his life.

Jack finally made his mark as a scholar in 1935 with the publication of *The Allegory of Love: A Study in*

Medieval Tradition. He had worked on it for ten years since the concept had been suggested to him by his English tutor in 1925. It was a study covering the forms of allegorical love poetry from the eleventh century's *The Romance of the Rose* to Spenser's *The Faerie Queene*, written in the sixteenth century.

The book received excellent reviews and a prestigious award, raising Lewis to the position of a medievalist scholar with few peers in the eyes of his Oxford contemporaries. Because of the book, Lewis was selected to write *The History of English Literature in the Sixteenth Century*, which was volume three of *The Oxford History of English Literature*.

By then Lewis was established as a leading scholar at Oxford. He was also president of various literary clubs. The first was the "Coalbiters," a group that read old Icelandic sagas in the original language and included J. R. R. Tolkien as its most renowned member. Later, Lewis would establish the "Socratic Club," creating a safe space for atheists and agnostics to engage Christians in no-holds-barred debate and dialogue.

Most significant and long lasting, however, was the "Inklings," made up primarily of Lewis's Christian friends including, among others, Owen Barfield, Charles Williams, Nevill Coghill, Lewis's personal physician, Dr. Humphrey Havard, Hugo Dyson, and J. R. R. Tolkien. They first met in Jack's rooms at Magdalen. Later, their meetings were held at a popular local pub called the Eagle and Child, known to Oxonians as "the Bird and Baby." About this group,

Lewis wrote, "Is any pleasure on earth as great as a circle of Christian friends by a fire?"

Lewis continued on this path—teaching, writing, taking long walks, meeting with various debating groups around Oxford—until the fall of 1939, when England entered World War II.

Other than a few shortages, the terrible war hardly impacted Lewis's lifestyle. More than forty years old, he was not expected to take up arms and fight. However, Warren, still in the reserves, was called up soon after the war began. Jack joined the Oxford Home Guard and took a weekly stint at protecting the town in case of invasion, which was a very real fear at the height of the war.

As London was struck night after night by German bombs, many children were evacuated to the countryside for safety. Always kind and hospitable, Mrs. Moore offered to take in such children at The Kilns. Naturally, Jack and Warnie agreed, seeing this as a Christian duty.

One of the evacuated children was intrigued by a large wardrobe in the hall and several times asked Lewis about it. Once she hid inside, where Lewis found her. This incident later gave him the idea for a children's book in which four youngsters enter a wardrobe only to exit from the other side into a strange land, there having many adventures. But the writing of the *Chronicles of Narnia* would not begin for another ten years.

During the war, Lewis's publisher asked him to write a book on pain and suffering. This work, entitled *The*

Problem of Pain, was published in 1940. It was a best-seller from the very start, reprinted year after year. *The Problem of Pain* is a brilliant exposition of the Christian belief in the mercy and judgment of God, but with a touch of sentiment. In it Lewis professed, "When pain is to be borne, a little courage helps more than knowledge, a little human sympathy more than courage." He was to add much on the subject when later confronted with the overwhelming suffering and death of his much-loved wife, Joy.

Following the publication of his controversial book *The Screwtape Letters,* C. S. Lewis became an overnight international celebrity. The idea came to him in Holy Trinity Church while Lewis was listening to an unusually dull sermon. The book consists of a collection of letters from an older devil, Screwtape, offering advice to his nephew, a younger devil named Wormwood. In each chapter, Screwtape instructs his nephew on how to snatch a Christian away from his newfound faith and win him for hell. The letters first appeared as a series in the *Guardian,* a Church of England weekly publication. Then they were published in England as a book in 1941 by Geoffrey Bles and in America in 1942 by Macmillan. The tongue-in-cheek letters were clever and novel, and the book became a huge success in America. Not quite as popular in England, the book caused a stir at Oxford. Stuffy professors considered it undignified to write about devils as though they actually existed. Many of the professors snubbed Lewis. But *Time* magazine considered *The Screwtape*

Letters important enough to earn C. S. Lewis a place on its cover with the subtitle: "His Heresy—Christian Orthodoxy."*

With its unusual insight and biting satire, *The Screwtape Letters* became a major religious book and brought in considerable royalties, which Lewis gave entirely away to the poor. As popular as ever, *The Screwtape Letters* is still read today at retreats and studied during Lent, and it continues to demonstrate how clever Satan can be at trapping Christians. Two million copies have been sold to date.

The book also caught the attention of the British Broadcasting Corporation. As World War II continued, and with London practically destroyed by nightly bombing by the Germans, the BBC looked for something to uplift its war-weary listeners. The producers thought of broadcasting some type of inspirational messages but thought words from a clergyman might be ignored. Noting the recent fame of *The Screwtape Letters,* whose author was a layperson in the religious field, they invited Lewis to write and broadcast several inspirational addresses to lift the morale of both soldiers and civilians, all of them continually at risk of injury or death.

At first Lewis was reticent about appearing on regular broadcasts, as he viewed radio as an infringement on people's private space and time. However, he eventually agreed to undertake a series of four fifteen-minute talks each Wednesday during August 1941.

---

*Time, vol. L, no. 10, September 8, 1947.

The broadcasts, entitled *Right and Wrong*, were an immediate success. Lewis's vitality, rich voice, and clear exposition of theology attracted more and more listeners. Many pub owners would turn up the radio when it was time for Lewis's evening talk and insist that everyone "quiet down to listen."

Given the widespread popularity of the first series, the BBC wanted Lewis to do more. The next series was entitled *What Christians Believe*. Lewis charted his talks carefully so as not to offend Christians of any persuasion and stressed doctrines common to all denominations.

Letters from listeners began to pour into the BBC studio. Lewis attempted to answer them all, a formidable task since he responded to each by hand. Soon, Warnie offered to help, typing the answers faster than Jack could and taking some of the burden off his brother. The talks were collected and eventually published as hardcover books and then in a single volume entitled *Mere Christianity*. The *Times Literary Supplement* wrote, "Mr. Lewis has a quite unique power of making theology attractive, exciting, and uproariously funny." The *New York Herald Tribune Book Review* stated, "His clarity of thought and simplicity of expression have a magic about them which makes plain the most abstruse problems of theological speculation."

By 1942 Lewis had made his mark on both the religious and scholarly worlds. Next he was to win the hearts of children everywhere with his tales of Narnia.

CHAPTER FIVE

OFF TO NARNIA

How could a stuffy professor, isolated from children during most of his life, write a series of books so attractive to children all over the world? And why did this eminent scholar, immersed in the classics and in medieval literature, suddenly decide to write in the entirely different field of children's books?

During the grim years of World War II, the Lewis brothers and Mrs. Moore took in children evacuated from bombed-out London. The Kilns was a perfect refuge for those seeking a haven from German aggression, with its big house, extensive grounds, fresh air, woods, pond, and tennis court. Ann, Martin, Rose, and Peter were the first children to arrive at The Kilns. This was Lewis's first exposure to children, living day and night amid their shouting, laughing, and crying.

Lewis's newfound Christian faith inspired him to speak of God to these young guests, especially since they were under such duress—separated from their parents, friends, and homes. Jack often entertained the children with stories he made up just for them.

With the war over in 1945, the children returned to their homes. Perhaps Lewis missed them; it seems that he wanted a way to communicate something of his own joy in Christ to other children.

Toward the close of the 1940s, Jack began writing *The Lion, the Witch, and the Wardrobe,* which became the first of the seven children's books that make up the *Chronicles of Narnia.* As mentioned earlier, it was the curiosity of a little girl evacuated to The Kilns that brought the wardrobe to center stage as the entrance to the enchanted land of Narnia. Lewis had almost completed the book when the character of Aslan the lion came literally bounding into a dream. Lewis had always been intrigued by the strength and majesty of lions and by the male lion's leadership. He went back and incorporated Aslan as the main character of the story and later used him in the subsequent books of the Narnia series.

Pleased with his first attempt at a children's book, Jack read the early chapters of the manuscript to his friends, the Inklings. To Jack's surprise, J. R. R. Tolkien found it dull and disjointed, a jumble of unrelated mythologies. He advised Lewis to abandon the effort. Jack was hurt and disappointed. But another friend and former student, Roger Lancelyn Green, author of a children's book entitled *The Wood That Time Forgot,* liked the story and urged Jack to complete it. Lewis finished writing the first volume in 1948 and dedicated it to Lucy Barfield, the young daughter of Owen Barfield, another close friend and fellow Inkling. Jack's publisher Geoffrey Bles was pleased to publish the book, hoping to capitalize on Lewis's growing fame.

The Lion, the Witch, and the Wardrobe became one of the most popular children's books ever written, and Geoffrey Bles encouraged Lewis to add additional volumes, which eventually numbered seven in all. Today, Lewis is more readily associated with his Narnia books, despite his fame as one of the leading Christian apologists of the twentieth century.

Lewis's whole life seemed to have prepared him to write these fantasies. As a young child, his only playmate was his older brother, Warnie. Jack was tutored at home by his mother and governess, so he never attended nursery school or kindergarten, never romped with boys his own age during recess.

In place of a small boy's usual activities, young Jack lived in a world of his own imagination, one filled with talking animals. Since earliest childhood, he had been a lover of myths, legends, and fairy tales. He particularly delighted in the age of chivalry, which explained his adult interest in both the courtly world of medieval literature and the knightly realm of Narnia itself. Narnia was a fantasyland full of imaginary creatures, flora, and fauna, as well as humans with all the foibles, weaknesses, and occasional courage found in all ages of history; but Narnia especially reflected the chivalric qualities of Lewis's beloved medieval world.

C. S. Lewis

Like most medieval tales, the Narnia adventures often feature a quest requiring a long, hazardous journey though difficult, unknown terrain and waters. The story line would often develop from images Lewis first saw in his dreams, as with Aslan. He never consciously employed characters or situations that were intentionally devised to teach Christian values or virtues. He felt that too many children were turned off by the overly preachy stories found all too often in Sunday school.

By contrasting good with evil, by pitting courage and kindness against cruelty and selfishness, by setting these themes in exciting stories of adventure, and by making his heroes and villains children, Jack created books that intrigued young readers. He felt that art should teach by delighting; he involved his youthful audience by enchanting them. This he certainly accomplished, for most children could hardly wait for the next Narnia book to come off the press.

Even if a reader never associated Aslan with Christ, he or she could not fail to realize that here was a godlike figure who represented good. Likewise, the four children who enter Narnia by way of the wardrobe behave in ways that are both good and bad. Peter, the leader, is full of hope and courage, while Susan is wary and cautious; Edmund is wily and treacherous, while Lucy is kindly and unselfish. Again and again in each book, these four face situations in which the right action may be painful and difficult. Throughout, we see the four grow wiser, stronger, and truer.

Are the books too violent, too filled with tragic consequences? Not for today's children, who watch hours of TV programs, many filled with sordid situations and violence for its own sake. In Lewis's books, the four children may fall into difficult straits, often with no promise of escape; yet they eventually overcome every challenge through the combined force of their own bravery and cleverness and the power and loving intervention of the great lion Aslan.

C. S. Lewis's Narnia books were published over a six-year period, between 1950 and 1956. The final book, *The Last Battle,* won the Carnegie Medal for the best book of that year. Lewis wrote each volume in less than three months. During that same period, he did many other things as well: carried out his teaching duties at Oxford; accepted an appointment as professor of medieval and renaissance literature at Magdalene College, Cambridge; wrote his autobiography, *Surprised by Joy;* and completed his highly acclaimed *History of English Literature in the Sixteenth Century.*

It was also during the early 1950s that Lewis first received a letter from an American author, Joy Davidman Gresham, who would become his wife before the decade was over. He dedicated *The Horse and His Boy,* number six in the Narnia series, to Joy's two young sons, David and Douglas.

All the time that he was writing and teaching, C. S. Lewis was under a severe strain at home, mainly because of his brother Warnie. Warnie had retired from the British army with the rank of major. Highly educated and talented like his brother, he too was the author of several books. He made his mark on the literary world in 1953 with his first volume on French history, *The Splendid Century*. The book had taken eleven years to write, but it made Major Lewis a recognized authority on the history of seventeenth-century France. He eventually published seven volumes on the world of Louis XIV. Warnie also helped his better-known brother with the voluminous mail that resulted from Jack's now extensive writings.

Sadly, through much of Warnie's later life, he suffered from alcoholism, which caused the rest of the household much concern and embarrassment. Although he made several attempts at recovery, the situation steadily worsened. Many a night Jack would tramp from pub to pub looking for his brother and then call a cab to get him home.

Mrs. Moore, now growing older and more troublesome to live with, also made life difficult for Jack. According to various friends and biographers, she treated Jack almost as a servant in their own home and frequently ordered him to assist in the kitchen or with housecleaning.

Perhaps as an act of humility or Christian discipline, Jack would put down whatever book he was reading or manuscript he was working on and dutifully jump up to assist her. Warnie wrote that she took advantage of Jack's good nature almost every half hour when he was home. As there were two maids in the house, Jack's help wasn't really necessary, but it seems the maids and Mrs.

Moore quarreled continuously. Living in a household with such quarrelsome women was difficult for both men, but it troubled Warnie the most. He had thrived on the orderliness and regularity of military life.

At vacation times, Jack and Warnie were justifiably happy to escape Mrs. Moore, taking long walking tours of Ireland and Wales. Both men delighted in the clean, fresh air of hill trails, swinging their walking sticks and fencing with words about history, literature, and theology. These were the most carefree of days, when the experiences of their boyhood bubbled forth and their love for each other deepened.

Jack never felt closer to God than when out-of-doors, admiring creation. Jack would praise God, both in his heart and outwardly, for the beauty of the hills, gardens, lakes, and especially the sea, which he had loved all his life. A loyal Irishman, he never doubted that the Irish were the best people and Ireland the best place.

As Mrs. Moore approached seventy, she became increasingly senile and began having problems with her legs, which made walking difficult. She turned over the job of walking her dog to Jack. He also carried Mrs. Moore's meals upstairs to her room when her legs were too weak to get her down to the dining room. Then in April 1950, Mrs. Moore fell out of bed several times. An ambulance took her to a nursing home in North Oxford; the doctor determined that she would have to remain there permanently.

Paying for Mrs. Moore's medical care placed a major financial burden on Lewis. He had planned a trip to

Ireland but had to cancel it due to the added expense. He visited Mrs. Moore at the nursing home every day, however, for he considered her his second mother. He never reneged on his promise to Paddy to take care of her.

Janie King Moore died of the flu January 23, 1951, at the age of seventy-nine. For thirty years, she had ruled The Kilns in an autocratic manner, behaving as though she were the sole owner. Yet, she had truly loved Jack in her own way the whole time.

After Mrs. Moore's death, Jack felt free to take his cancelled vacation. He called on Arthur Greeves, still his closest friend and confidant, to join him. Arthur made the plans and reservations, and the two men toured their favorite places in Ireland. Jack called 1952 the happiest year of his life. He was free to take trips with Warnie or to go to Malvern to visit with his former student, now dear friend and future biographer, George Sayer. And at home there was no strident voice breaking in on his thoughts or work.

But it would not be long before someone new would come into Jack's life—Joy Davidman Gresham.

CHAPTER SIX

AND JOY CAME IN

For thirty years, one woman had dominated C. S. Lewis's life. Now she was gone. Although Mrs. Moore had been bossy and acted like a domineering mother toward Jack, her absence left The Kilns empty and different.

At first the two bachelors tried to take care of the house themselves. It was a disaster. The food was inedible, and The Kilns soon became a total mess. Warnie decided they would have to hire a housekeeper, and the brothers settled on Mrs. Miller, a plump, balding woman of middle age. She would remain with them for the rest of their lives.

Meanwhile, Jack had become increasingly famous as a writer of fiction, literary history, and Christian apologetics. Piles of letters from his admirers arrived daily. He made an attempt to answer them all, which cut deeply into his time for teaching and writing. When he was able, Warnie helped with the correspondence.

One evening Warnie and Jack were in the common room. Warnie was pecking away at his ancient typewriter, and Jack was writing letters in his neat controlled scrawl.

Warnie stopped. "Jack," he began, "aren't you spending too much time answering letters? Who are you writing now?"

Jack wrinkled his forehead and set down his pen. "Perhaps I do spend a lot of time on letters, but some of these people have severe problems. When they ask for help, I feel duty-bound to give it. Take this lady, for instance, an American with two young boys. Her husband doesn't understand her and is very abusive. She is thinking of leaving him, but she's just become a Christian and wants my advice on what to do."

"Oh Jack, why get mixed up in a family squabble?" asked Warren. "You say she's just become a Christian; what was she before?"

"A Communist and a Jew," replied Jack, leaning over to refill his pipe. "Strange situation. She's married to a writer. She's an author, too. Wrote a novel."

Warnie appeared more interested. "A writer? What's her name? Have I heard of her?"

Jack shook his head. "I doubt it. Her name is Joy, Joy Gresham, but she publishes under her maiden name of Davidman. I think the title of her book is *Anya*. It's about Jewish peasants in her family's native land."

Not long after that, Mrs. Gresham wrote again, informing Jack that she would be visiting England soon and suggesting that they meet. Jack never suspected that anything would come of their meeting, but he could not have been more mistaken. Joy Davidman Gresham was soon to become the most important person in his life.

No two people could have been more different nor have come from such opposite backgrounds as Jack, an Oxford-educated British gentleman—reserved, reflective, conservative—and Joy, equally brilliant but brash, deeply rooted in the radical tradition, and a former communist from the Bronx.

Joy's parents, Joe and Jen Davidman, were Jewish immigrants from Eastern Europe. Joy's father, Joseph Isaac Davidman, was born in Poland but came to New York City in 1893 as a six-year-old boy. The Davidmans lived in a tenement on the Lower East Side, where Joseph's father earned a living as a pushcart peddler and later worked in the garment industry. Their home was dominated by old-world Jewish customs.

Later, Joseph Davidman left his orthodox faith, trying socialism instead. He worked his way through the City College of New York, becoming a teacher and eventually a junior high school principal. Joy's mother, Jeannette Spivack, was also a graduate of City College and a teacher. She came from a more financially substantial Jewish background in Odessa, Russia. Her family took little or no interest in the Jewish faith, abandoning its practices shortly after their arrival in America.

The two met in college and were married in 1909. As both held well-paying teaching jobs, they were soon able to move to the respectable neighborhood of the Grand Concourse in the Bronx. They soon found their way into America's fast-growing middle class. Their first child, Joy, born April 18, 1915, profited from that. She attended good public schools, graduating from Evander Childs High School when she was only fourteen. Her IQ was the highest yet recorded there. Her parents provided Joy with a grand piano and many years of lessons. Their son Howard, born four years later, was able to attend medical school and eventually became a psychiatrist.

At Hunter College, Joy, still a teenager, made a strong impact with her writing talent. She had a photographic memory and could quote everything she read. Like C. S. Lewis, she was not only exceptionally intelligent but also a voracious reader of poetry, history, and the classics.

Only five feet two inches tall, Joy was plump and plain, except for her dark hair and eyes. She had no sense of fashion and dressed carelessly. Jack would be drawn to her not by her looks but by her extraordinary mind, assertiveness, and quick wit.

During her childhood, Joy suffered from several severe illnesses: scarlet fever, hyperinsulinism, and an overactive thyroid. Instead of surgically removing her malfunctioning thyroid, the doctors treated it with radium. Joy wore a radium belt around her neck for a year. Today, it is thought that this extended exposure to radium may have caused the cancer that later resulted in her early death.

Joy majored in English at Hunter, where she was appointed associate editor of *Echo,* the college magazine. *Echo* published some of her poems and short stories. "Apostate," her story of a Russian Jewess who turned Christian, won the Hunter College Short Story Award. A poem, "Reveal the Titan," also published in *Echo,* foreshadowed her struggle between materialism and Christianity.

But first Joy turned to Communism. With no religion in the home of her youth, the teenage girl looked for something to believe in. The Great Depression of the 1930s left her disillusioned with capitalism. Joy saw people starving, some committing suicide, families being thrown out on the street with nowhere to go. She saw "Hoovervilles" in the parks and widespread unemployment. All of these conditions degraded both the educated and the blue-collar man.

Too young to teach, Joy enrolled for graduate study following her graduation from Hunter. In the summer of 1935, at the age of twenty, she received a master's degree in English literature from Columbia. She taught English in two high schools but continued to live at home to reduce her expenses. Soon dissatisfied with conditions at both schools, Joy resigned, using her free time to write.

Encouraged when several of her poems were published in an important poetry magazine, Joy collected fifty of them in a book she called *Letter to a Comrade.* Published by Yale University Press in 1938, the small volume received excellent reviews and sold quite well.

It is still in print sixty years later. The book made such an impact that Joy was taken on by an important New York agent, Brandt and Brandt. The book also received a thousand-dollar award from the National Institute of Arts and Letters, an honor she shared with Robert Frost, who would later become one of America's most celebrated poets.

Through her editor, Pulitzer–Prize-winning author Stephen Vincent Benét, Joy was invited to the MacDowell Colony in Peterborough, New Hampshire. There, for four delightful summers, she hobnobbed with the creative geniuses of mid-twentieth-century America: literary giants such as Willa Cather and Louis Untermeyer, as well as many well-known composers and artists.

At MacDowell Joy completed her first novel, *Anya,* published by Macmillan in 1940. It was based on a story her Russian mother had told her. The review in the *New York Times* called it "a powerful, well-written novel."

At MacDowell, Joy also came in contact with many writers and musicians who belonged to, or had leanings toward, the American Communist Party. Some of her former college friends had already joined. Joy described what drew her to the party: "Maybe no rational person would worry about the rest of the world. I found myself worrying all the same. I wanted to do something, so I joined the Communist Party." This she did during a huge rally at Madison Square Garden. No sooner was Joy a card-carrying member of the American Communist Party than she was put to work as a writer on its publication, *New Masses*. There she evaluated and edited manuscripts and became their poetry and book critic. Joy relished the power this gave her, even though it was an unpaid volunteer position.

In 1939 she went west to spend six months in Hollywood writing movie scripts. Unfortunately, not one of her efforts ever made it to the screen. Disappointed, she returned to New York and resumed her work at *New Masses*, editing manuscripts, writing reviews of books and films, and acting as poetry editor. However, now she was taken on as a full-time paid member of the staff, with a salary of twenty-five dollars per week.

It was at a Communist Party meeting in New York that Joy met her first husband, William Lindsay Gresham, a southerner and lapsed Christian. At that time, Bill Gresham was a freelance writer who had fought against the Fascists in the Spanish Civil War and had later become a lukewarm member of the Communist Party.

After a short courtship, the couple married in August 1942, when Joy was twenty-seven. This was a second marriage for Bill, who had earlier married and divorced a New York socialite. He had lived off his first wife's wealth while writing, working for a while at the *New York Evening Post* and later at an advertising agency. When none of this turned into the success he craved, Gresham left both job and wife to fight for the Communists in the Spanish Civil War.

Upon his return, the tall, lean, rather sensual war veteran was totally disillusioned and drowned his remorse in alcohol. In 1942 he even tried to hang himself, after which his shaken first wife divorced him. Shortly afterward Bill and Joy were married by a justice of the peace in Peterborough, New Hampshire. A reception was held at the nearby MacDowell Colony, where both had many friends. Joy's parents and brother attended, even though her parents were shocked and hurt that she had married a Gentile, who, moreover, lacked any resources to support their talented daughter.

Joy and Bill moved into a tiny apartment on New York's Lower East Side. From the very beginning, it was obvious that they were totally mismatched. They argued frequently. Bill drank and moped, while Joy supported them on her twenty-five-dollar-a-week salary at *New Masses*. When Bill went for psychoanalysis, their small income was stretched even more.

Joy soon discovered she was pregnant, and the Greshams moved into a three-room apartment in Queens, where their first child, David, was born in March of 1944. Seventeen months later, in November of 1945, a second child, Douglas, was born.

By then World War II was over. America was enjoying a new prosperity, with jobs for everyone. People were buying new cars, and housing developments were springing up all over. It was a brave new world.

Joy wanted something better, too. She and Bill took their little family out of the city to Ossining, a pleasant country area on the Hudson River, twenty miles north of New York City. Bill commuted to his newfound advertising job in the city.

But Joy had another reason for leaving New York—Bill was having an affair. To make matters worse, he soon suffered a nervous breakdown.

One day Bill phoned Joy from his office to tell her that he was "falling apart" and that "his mind was going." He wasn't coming home. Alone in Ossining with the babies, Joy had nowhere to turn. Her parents had advised her against marrying Bill; she was ashamed to call now to ask them for help. Bill's unfaithfulness was devastating to Joy; her own parents had always been true to each other. This was not what she had anticipated from the marriage, especially so soon. How would she support herself and care for two sons alone? Where could she turn? To whom?

Alone and on her knees, here is how Joy described her conversion: "There was a person with me in that room," she wrote, "directly present to my consciousness, a person so real that all my previous life was by comparison a mere shadow play. And I myself was more alive than I had ever been. It was like waking from sleep." The experience changed her life. She later exclaimed, "I was the most surprised atheist ever!"

Several days later, Bill came home to find his wife a different woman. She appeared serene and gentler and admitted to weaknesses in her own personality: arrogance, prejudices, and vindictiveness. Joy set about trying to change. At first she embraced Judaism but soon found that the "faith of her fathers" was not fulfilling.

At the same time, the Greshams' fortunes took an unexpected turn for the better. A book Bill had been working on for years, *Nightmare Alley*, was published. Bill received a cash advance and royalties from the book, which carried them along comfortably for a while and helped pay off their debts.

Bill's agent sold the book to Hollywood for sixty-thousand dollars. Neither Joy nor Bill had ever possessed so much money. What to do with it? Both Greshams wanted a place to call their own, to put down roots somewhere in a country setting. They found their dream home in Staatsburg, Dutchess County. It was a large two-story house with tall white columns set on thirty-eight wooded acres. Both felt this was the perfect place to raise their two lively boys.

In 1950, the four Greshams moved in to their new home, bringing Joy's grand piano and hundreds of books. Joy set out a vegetable garden and canned vegetables and fruits. Bill looked forward to an idyllic life as a country gentleman writer. The whole family joined the nearby Presbyterian church, where Joy and the boys were baptized.

Joy began immersing herself in the Bible and in books on Christian living. It was then that she stumbled on the writings of C. S. Lewis. She quickly realized her beliefs were much closer to those of the Episcopal Church, and the family transferred membership to a nearby parish.

After reading Lewis's books *The Screwtape Letters* and *Miracles,* Joy realized she had many unanswered questions that she wanted to ask the author. At first she refrained from writing Lewis, perhaps from embarrassment or shyness. Meanwhile, she and Bill became very close friends with Chad Walsh, an Episcopal priest and writer. Father Walsh had recently spent several months in England interviewing Lewis for a biography that he was working on. It had been published by Macmillan in 1949 as *C. S. Lewis: Apostle to the Skeptics.* Father Walsh urged Joy to write Lewis, assuring her that Lewis would most likely respond.

Joy mailed her first letter to Lewis in January 1950, and soon she and the Oxford don were engaged in active correspondence. With each new answer to her ever deeper questions, Joy's faith grew and blossomed. Meanwhile, Bill's faith ebbed and died. First, he turned to Dianetics and then to Zen-Buddhism, Tarot cards, and I-Ching, moving further and further away from the Christian faith. Their marriage seemed headed toward disaster.

Joy fell sick with a liver infection, which led to jaundice and a notable weight loss. Too ill to care for herself, her home, or her children, she spent weeks in bed reading. During her illness, Bill was hardly ever sober and did little to help. Sometimes, he became violent.

In addition, he continued to have extramarital affairs, which Joy found demeaning and difficult to handle.

Then a new element entered their troubled lives, an element that eventually destroyed their marriage. Renée Pierce, a cousin of Joy's, had run away from her own alcoholic husband and moved in with the Greshams. She brought her two young children, Bob and Rose Mary, with her. At first the two families melded together rather well. Joy loved to cook but hated housework; Renée, on the other hand, was neat by nature and didn't mind cleaning, washing, and ironing. It was not too long, however, before Bill was deeply attracted to Renée and again betrayed his marriage to Joy.

As a Christian, Joy felt she could not divorce Bill and did everything possible to keep their marriage afloat. As matters appeared increasingly hopeless, she resolved to go to England.

The trip would serve several purposes: It would provide Joy needed refreshment, as she was still recovering from her illness; it would give her the opportunity to find an English publisher for *Smoke on the Mountain,* her new book on the Ten Commandments and her first since becoming a Christian; it would allow her time and space to reflect on her marriage; and it would also provide her with the opportunity to meet C. S. Lewis in person, in the hope that he might be able to advise her on her situation.

CHAPTER SEVEN

LOVE AND MARRIAGE

Joy sailed alone to England in August of 1952. Accompanied by a friend from London, she first met Jack for tea early in September at the Eastgate Hotel in Oxford. Jack had also brought a friend along, George Sayer, his former student and future biographer. In December Joy was invited to return for a visit with Jack and Warnie over a weekend at The Kilns. Jack was intrigued by Joy's bold, brilliant conversation. He had never met a woman like her before. She remained in England six months, until January 1953.

With Joy away in England, Bill and Renée became more involved with each other. It was not long before Bill decided he would divorce Joy and marry Renée. Joy returned to New York only to find herself in an even worse situation.

Months later, Jack received another letter from her. This one was quite alarming. Joy reported that she had been physically assaulted by her husband, who was going through difficult times financially. It seemed that the IRS was dunning him for back taxes. She lived in fear that Bill might injure her or their two little boys, David and Douglas. To escape, she planned to move to England. She loved England and was disenchanted with America. She would move to London, perhaps permanently.

Warren warned Jack, "Now look what's happened because of all those letters. That woman expects you to take care of her, plus her sons. I figured something like this might happen."

In November 1953, Joy Gresham, now divorced, boarded the *Britannia* and sailed for Liverpool with her two boys, Douglas and David, then eight and nine years old. The ship was small and old and rocked mercilessly throughout the eight-day voyage. David was sick the entire trip, but Douglas loved every minute of it, racing about the deck, awed by the ship's great engines and entranced by a tour of the bridge.

At last, the threesome arrived in gray, dreary Liverpool. Alone in a new land, with little money, the three Greshams rented two rooms in London at 14 Bellsize Park Avenue, where they would live for the next eighteen months. Jack generously offered to help with expenses and arranged to enroll the boys at Dane Court School.

Just before Christmas, Jack invited Joy and her sons to visit The Kilns for a long weekend. Both boys had read and loved the Narnia books. They had not accompanied their mother on her first trip to England and were excited about meeting the celebrated author.

Joy, too, looked forward to seeing Jack again. By then they had been corresponding for several years. They each delighted in the other's sharp wit and knowledge of literature and history. Both loved and wrote poetry.

The Greshams took the train to Oxford and then a bus to Headington. They walked up Kilns Lane to the Lewis brothers' home. As they approached the two-story country house, they walked through a landscape of woods, lawns, and flower beds. Joy straightened the boys' caps and ties and then knocked on the green door.

Mrs. Miller appeared and ushered the Greshams into the common room, a large room with a fireplace where the Lewises spent much of their time. Jack and Warnie rushed in to greet the Greshams, taking Joy's coat and the boys' caps. Douglas and David stood awkwardly until Warnie suggested that Mrs. Miller take them to the kitchen for tea and biscuits. Douglas was surprised to discover that the famous author of the Narnia series was not the tall, dashing knight he had expected. Rather, he found C. S. Lewis to be portly and rather shabbily dressed. Cigarette ashes covered his jacket and his shoes were worn and dusty. Clearly, the adventures Lewis wrote about must have come exclusively from his imagination and not personal experience. Douglas hid his disappointment and followed Mrs. Miller into the warm and fragrant kitchen.

For Joy Gresham, however, Jack Lewis was anything but a stout middle-aged professor. He was a savior and hero who had helped to stabilize them financially, settled them in London, and paid the boys' school tuition.

The funds came from a charitable trust that Owen Barfield, his friend and attorney, had set up from Lewis's book royalties. Jack preferred to live simply— the old-fashioned way. He spent most of his royalties on the needy, especially young people unable to pay for their education.

The next day, the Lewises and their guests took a long walk around the property, passed the small pond, and then hiked through the countryside. The boys ran ahead through the trees, with Joy, Jack, and Warnie talking and laughing behind. Later, visiting Magdalen College, where Lewis was a fellow, the boys were privileged to climb its famous tower and pat the resident deer.

Too soon the wonderful visit was over. The Greshams returned to their small flat in London; Jack collapsed into his chair, exhausted from trying to keep up with the two youngsters. After the holidays, David and Douglas were sent off to Dane Court, a boarding school in Surrey. Eight-year-old Doug was dreadfully homesick. To make matters worse, he was also teased unmercifully because of his American accent. He quickly affected an English accent and fought readily with any schoolmate who mocked his speech.

In August 1955, everything changed for the better. Jack found a charming duplex for the Greshams at 10 Old High Street in Headington. The house had plenty of space, with an upstairs bedroom for each. Now only minutes away from The Kilns, Jack and Warnie popped in frequently. Joy attracted the Lewises like a magnet. Jack so enjoyed her ability to make him laugh. He also liked her brash, brilliant, and often outrageous comments. But, for all this, Joy was not much liked by his university friends.

When she had first traveled to England in 1952, she was thirty-seven and Jack was fifty-four, a seventeen-year difference in age. Both had seen success as writers, but Lewis had become world famous. During that first trip, Jack helped Joy with *Smoke on the Mountain,* her book on the Ten Commandments. He not only made suggestions; he also wrote a glowing introduction. Now published and a modest success, the book provided Joy with royalty checks of her own, although they were not enough to support herself and the boys. She earned needed additional money typing Lewis's manuscripts.

By 1954 C. S. Lewis had been a fellow of Magdalen for thirty years. During all that time, whether out of professional envy or resentment at his outspoken Christian views, he had never been offered a professorship or even an increase in salary. Many at Oxford considered this a disgrace, as Lewis's work was admired internationally. Jack, too, was troubled by this neglect and increasingly found his work as a tutor to be less desirable and fulfilling.

Then something happened to bring about a drastic change in his life. Some friends brought Lewis's dissatisfaction to the attention of Cambridge University's English faculty. As a result, a professorship of medieval and renaissance studies was created by Cambridge just for him. Jack gratefully accepted the position, even though Oxford countered with an offer of a full professorship. But Oxford had made the offer too late.

Jack didn't want to leave The Kilns and move to Cambridge. His solution was to stay at Cambridge from Tuesday through Friday, when school was in term, and to live at home over the weekends and holidays. The new position also included a generous increase in salary, which Jack needed to continue supporting Joy and her sons.

On November 29, 1954, Professor Lewis presented his inaugural lecture at Cambridge University to a hall jammed with colleagues, enthusiastic students, and friends. He received a tremendous ovation.

Jack didn't move into his rooms at Cambridge until January of 1955. He dreaded change of any sort. Joy helped him with the move, lugging books and furniture from Oxford to Cambridge.

At Cambridge, with few classes to teach, Jack found ample time to write, but ideas failed to come as easily as before. Joy began to encourage him on those days when he was back at The Kilns. The two tossed a variety of ideas around. One day Jack had a flash of inspiration, and from it came *Till We Have Faces,* the book he liked most of all his writings. Joy helped with the editing and typing, and Jack, in turn, paid her for the work she did. The arrangement might have continued indefinitely had it not been for a very important and unexpected letter that arrived from the British government.

Upon reading the letter, Joy learned that her visa had expired. She was told she could no longer work or live in England and was ordered to leave at once.

How could she leave? The boys were settled in their school. All three of the Greshams loved England and had no desire to return to the United States. Joy had nothing and no one in America to return to.

There seemed to be only one solution. If Jack married Joy, she would instantly become a British citizen and could remain in England permanently. Jack was willing to undergo a purely civil ceremony to provide Joy and the boys with British citizenship. It would not be a true Christian marriage but simply a legal formality that was to be kept secret.

Joy was agreeable, although by now she was actually in love with the famous professor and would have preferred a church wedding. But that could not be since the Church of England did not permit a divorced person to remarry.

On April 23, 1956, Joy and Jack were married at the Oxford Registry Office in a short civil ceremony. It was just a marriage of convenience, intended only to allow Joy and her sons to stay in England as British citizens. The three Greshams would continue to live at 10 Old High Street, and Joy would still be known as Mrs. Gresham.

Warnie felt uncomfortable, fearing at first he might come between Jack and Joy. He offered to leave The Kilns and find other lodgings, but the others wouldn't hear of it. Warnie was almost as fond of Joy as Jack was, and the boys enjoyed his jovial company. Nothing would change, or so they all thought.

Plans were made for the three Greshams to move into The Kilns for the summer holiday of 1956. The summer passed, during which Joy complained of a severe pain in her hip. But she bravely saw to it that the boys had fun on their vacation.

Douglas swam and fished in the pond on the Lewis property. Jack tutored David in Latin and Greek. It seemed an ideal time, as the two families bonded together. Jack bought Douglas a horse and built a stable for it on the property.

Summer passed too quickly. David and Douglas returned to their prep school for the fall term, and Joy returned to her duplex on Old High Street.

It was not long afterward, on a day when Joy was alone in her lodgings, that she fell and was unable to get up. She telephoned for help. An ambulance was called, and Joy was rushed to nearby Wingfield Orthopedic Hospital. X-rays revealed that her left femur had been broken, but not from the fall. It had been eaten away by cancer. The disease was also detected in other areas of her body, including the left breast.

Joy underwent three operations, followed by radiation treatments. Although in severe pain, she maintained a courageous, optimistic manner.

Because of the seriousness of their mother's condition, David and Douglas were immediately summoned home from school to visit her in the hospital. Initially they were told only that she had broken her leg. It became Jack's task to tell the two young boys that their mother had cancer. At this time, Douglas was eleven. When he entered the room, the sight of his mother tore at his heart. She was propped up in bed, her hair held back by two white ribbons. Her eyes were sunken in dark circles. Her skin had a sickly and sallow color. Fear pierced the youngster. Was she going to die? He hadn't seen his father in years. "Will I be an orphan?" he wondered.

After the brief, awkward visit, Douglas left to walk the mile home to The Kilns. His path led him on a lane past Holy Trinity, the church Jack attended. The boy entered and walked up the aisle to the altar rail. There he knelt and begged, "Please God, spare my mother's life."

As Douglas rose to his feet, he felt the fear lift and knew, as well as he knew anything, that God had heard his prayer.

In the meantime, Jack was struggling with a flood of unexpected emotions. For the first time, the confirmed bachelor of fifty-eight knew the pangs of love. As Joy lay in the hospital, his feelings swiftly deepened. Joy had cherished Jack since they first began corresponding, but he was only now beginning to realize that he loved her—just as he might possibly lose her forever.

Suddenly, Jack wanted something more than the Registry's mere civil marriage. He wanted the church to bless their union so that they would be married in the sight of God before Joy died. Due to Joy's serious condition, he went directly to the Bishop of Oxford to request the special dispensation needed for Jack to marry a divorced woman.

Bishop Carpenter welcomed Jack into his study.

"Come in, Jack. What a pleasure to see you. Do sit down. And how are you enjoying your post at Cambridge?"

"Very well, thank you, Your Grace. But that's not why I've come. I need your help. I've been seeing an American lady, Mrs. Joy Gresham, a divorcée. We would like to enter into the sacrament of marriage with the blessing of the church. I realize we need your permission first, which is why I'm here today. Mrs. Gresham is seriously ill with cancer. She is not expected to live."

The Bishop tugged at his collar. His face reddened. He was obviously uncomfortable. "I wish I could help you, Jack, but the Church of England does not sanction the marriage of divorced communicants. Certainly, of all people, you must be aware of that. I sympathize with your situation, but it is simply not in my power to grant a priest of my diocese permission to unite the two of you in the sacrament of Holy Matrimony."

Jack restrained from expressing his frustration. "In that case," he said solemnly, "it's best that I leave. Thank you for your time." He walked out and returned to The Kilns.

That night Lewis wrote to an old pupil, the Reverend Peter Bide. He had heard that Father Bide was a healer and asked him to come to the hospital and lay hands on Joy. Many people had been healed through this devout priest's ministrations.

Father Bide arrived at The Kilns. Before leaving for the hospital, Jack Lewis told Father Bide of his and Joy's great desire to be married according to the rite of the Church of England and in the sight of God. Jack explained that Joy was divorced but that, according to canon law, she had never really been married to William Gresham because Bill had already been married and divorced before he met Joy. This made her marriage to Bill invalid. In view of this, Father Bide agreed to marry Jack and Joy the very next day, following his prayers for Joy's healing.

On March 21, 1957, at 11 A.M., Jack, the floor nurse, and Father Bide gathered in Joy's hospital room. After they each received holy communion, the Anglican priest performed the marriage ceremony joining Jack and Joy as man and wife. No two people could have been happier.

CHAPTER EIGHT

THREE YEARS OF HAPPINESS, 1957–1960

"Now that you are better," Jack said to Joy, "you'll soon be released from the hospital. I think it best that you recuperate at The Kilns."

Joy looked up at her new husband, her face glowing with happiness. "Oh, Jack, you know I'll be OK at home."

"None of that," said Jack seriously. "I can't let you go back there alone. The doctor says you will need constant care. You must live at The Kilns. Warnie and I will care for you—we'll hire a nurse, too."

While waiting for the doctor to release Joy from the hospital, Jack turned the common room at The Kilns into a special room for her. He ordered a hospital bed and hired a trained nurse.

The day that Joy went home by ambulance was a great day for everyone. Jack's friends rallied around to help. They knew the two usually boisterous boys would make extra work for Jack and very likely create too much commotion for someone so seriously ill. Both Douglas and David were attending boarding school at Dane Court but had month-long holidays at Christmas and Easter. Mrs. Moore's daughter, now married to the violinist Leonard Blake, invited David and Douglas for one holiday at her home in Malvern. Douglas loved the hills of Malvern, the same countryside where Jack had been so unhappy at school many years earlier. The boys played squash and tumbled down the sheep-filled meadows.

Another family, friends of the Blakes, owned a seaside hotel at Ramsgate and invited the boys for the spring holiday. The owner, Mary Berners-Price, had two young daughters. Douglas promptly fell in love with both.

Meanwhile, Jack developed a severe pain in his back and, after several tests, was diagnosed as having osteoporosis, a softening of the bones. Even though it was sometimes so severe as to make him scream in pain, Jack was grateful that Joy had been relieved of her own terrible suffering.

As Joy became well enough to leave the common room, her eyes were opened to the shabbiness of The Kilns. Longtime bachelors, Jack and Warnie had let the place fall into total disrepair. Paint was chipping off the walls both inside and out. The designs on the rugs were obliterated by ashes dropped everywhere by the two chain-smoking owners. The ceilings were stained dark brown with the smoke of nicotine and many fires. Sofas and chairs had worn through to the springs, with the stuffing peeking out through the holes.

Now that Joy was to be mistress of The Kilns, she was determined to make it more livable. She perked up tremendously as she tackled the job of redoing everything. Her goal was to make the place reflect Jack's position as a professor at Cambridge. She hired painters, upholsterers, and roofers. She had the plumbing and electrical wiring redone and had central heating added to the damp, cold house. The kitchen was modernized with a gas stove and refrigerator.

The next time Douglas and David came home on holiday, they were delighted with the improvements. The Kilns now seemed more like an American home, with all the comforts they had been accustomed to.

Even more delightful for the boys was their mother's great improvement. She was now able to walk with the help of a cane. Joy became herself again, making wise-cracks and entering into conversations and arguments with Jack's literary friends. The Kilns was filled with laughter and contentment. Jack wrote to his dearest friend, "All that matters is that I'm in love. At times I'm tempted to think it's a double miracle. Recovery for her, and for me the love that passed me by in youth and in middle age."

Next, Joy tackled the garden. The gardener, Fred Paxford, also doubled as handyman and driver. He did his best with the grounds but was not creative. Joy designed flower beds and vegetable plots and had a

fence installed to keep out intruders. The place began to look more like a proper country estate than an abandoned derelict.

By January 1958, Joy's condition was termed "arrested" by her doctors. She was no longer in pain and even went for drives in the countryside.

Joy's refurbishing didn't stop with the house and garden. She took the famed Professor Lewis to town and had him buy new clothes and shoes, disposing of his comfortable but shabby attire. She wanted him to look as respectable as his reputation deserved. She even straightened out his financial affairs, showing him that he could afford to live better and was not on the edge of financial ruin, a fear he had inherited from his frugal father.

On sunny summer days, Joy would sit out in her garden and knit or crochet. Jack would sit beside her, hardly able to believe he was experiencing such happiness. Married life agreed with the lifelong bachelor. The rented hospital bed was returned and the happy couple now shared a bedroom upstairs.

Joy was an excellent cook, whereas the Lewis's housekeeper, Mrs. Miller, was not. As Joy gained strength and mobility, she taught Mrs. Miller some of her fancier dishes. Soon, delicious aromas came wafting from the tiny kitchen, and meals became a delight.

Joy even entertained. On the day of a dinner party at The Kilns, Douglas would polish the silver while David vacuumed the house and swept the walks. Later,

Douglas would set the table with fine china from Little Lea, the old Lewis home in Northern Ireland.

At seven o'clock, the guests would arrive, usually old friends from Jack's Oxford days, like George Sayer and Dr. Humphrey Havard, Lewis's longtime friend and personal physician. Austin Farrer, principal of Keble College, Oxford, would also attend. After drinks in the common room, the guests would move to the dining room. There they'd be taken aback by the newly decorated room, now clean, bright, and elegant with the drapes and carpets Joy had ordered. The lively party would enjoy a delicious dinner, all the while discussing their new works or recent travels and tossing clever banter back and forth. In later years, Douglas would say that any dinner at The Kilns was an education in itself. He commented that he learned more on any one evening at the table than he ever had at school.

Over the years, Jack had kept up his correspondence with Arthur Greeves and yearned to return to Ireland, the land of his birth. Jack also wanted to show Ireland to his bride. As both were in better health during the spring of 1958, they made plans to travel that summer.

Jack had never been on an airplane before and was nervous about flying. But once he and Joy were up in the sky, he was thrilled with his bird's-eye view of the land and Irish Sea below.

They were met at the airport by Arthur. Jack was proud to introduce his wife to his closest friend. Arthur drove the couple to their hotel and, throughout that week, took them to explore Donegal and other parts of the Emerald Isle, all in perfect weather. Joy was charmed by the thatched-roof cottages, the peat, and the heather. Nothing could have been more alien to a New Yorker than this simple, pastoral environment; yet, she took great pleasure in rural places, much preferring them over city life, which she hated.

On their return, Lewis taught at Cambridge during the week, leaving Joy alone at The Kilns. On an outing to her favorite restaurant, Studley Priory, Joy made a new friend, Jean Wakeman, who, like Joy, also walked painfully with a cane, but as the result of an injury at birth.

Miss Wakeman was a professional journalist who road-tested new automobiles and then reported on them for motor magazines. She invited Joy along on some of her midweek jaunts. The two would drive through the beautiful English countryside in a brand-new car, sleeping in quaint inns along the way. They roamed around the country, Joy commenting on the car from a passenger's perspective.

One time, when the boys were on holiday, Joy and Jean took them along for the ride. The four stayed in Solva, a fishing village in the south of Wales, where they roomed in a small pub frequented by local lobstermen. Douglas and David had a superb time going out to sea on the lobster boats, helping the men bait the pots and retrieve the lobsters. The boys climbed up the steep cliffs along the sea, clinging to crevices with their fingernails. Once they took a boat to a small island off the coast. On landing, Douglas ran off to find the island's only horse, which had swum there from the mainland long ago. Much too soon their vacation was over, but Douglas never forgot it. Years later, he would return to that nostalgic spot after he was grown and married.

The Kilns was now a paradise for the boys, a place of wonder and exploration. After several years of living in small apartments and duplexes, they were thrilled to run free through the grounds of the estate. In summer they fished and swam in the small pond that was part of the property. Jack bought Douglas a kayak with which to paddle around. In winter Douglas used Jack's boyhood skates to glide across the iced-over pond.

In the woods surrounding The Kilns lived pigeons, rabbits, and foxes, which the boys sometimes chased or shot with a gun. Douglas also liked to help Paxford with the garden. While digging and fertilizing, he became close friends with the family's rugged gardener.

Douglas also felt great admiration for his stepfather. After all, he was none other than the author of the beloved *Chronicles of Narnia*. Jack had even dedicated one of the books in the series, *The Horse and His Boy*, to David and Douglas.

Both boys had found love and stability at The Kilns. Even though Jack was not a demonstrative man, he showed his love by the attention he gave the boys. Jack talked to them about life, love, and the health of their mother. He paid their tuition at boarding school, making sure they had proper school uniforms and adequate spending money. Best of all for the Gresham boys was the knowledge that their mother was loved and cared for.

In 1959 Jack and Joy took another trip to Ireland, this time staying with Arthur. Joy appeared to be in perfect health except for a decided limp, the result of her cancer surgery, which left one leg shorter than the other. Jack and Joy later took the boys on a second holiday, in Wales. By all appearances, Joy seemed recovered. Her cure was thought to be truly miraculous.

But once back in England, Joy again experienced pain in her bad leg. She was taken to the hospital for treatment. Much to their surprise and profound alarm, they learned that the cancer had returned, this time in her right breast. She immediately underwent surgery again.

Joy was released from the hospital on May 2. Once more she had to use the wheelchair, but at least she was able to move around enough to take over the running of the house again. During the week, when Jack was at Cambridge, Warren pushed Joy's wheelchair down to the pond or into the garden, where she would check her flowers. On weekends, Jack took her to dinner at Studley Priory.

Bill Gresham, Douglas and David's father by birth, wrote to Joy demanding that his sons be returned to live with him after her death. Jack was furious and replied to Bill directly: "You have tortured one who is already on the rack. There is nothing Joy dreads so much as a return of her boys to your charge." Joy had told Jack about Bill Gresham's drunken behavior. The boys remembered him as a violent man who fired rifles through ceilings, threw chairs, and once broke a bottle over Douglas's head.

Lewis threatened to place every legal obstacle in Bill's way if he did not relent. The boys did not want to return to America or to the care of their troubled father.

Increasingly aware that she had little time left, Joy asked Jack to give her the gift of a holiday, a short trip to Greece. Not long after—with the encouragement of friends Roger and June Green, who would be their traveling companions—they made their way to Greece by air. The ten-day trip would prove idyllic. Joy seemed in perfect health, climbing the steep hill of the Acropolis to view the Parthenon. They basked in the warm Greek sun, so comforting to those accustomed to the colder north.

The happy couple took several side trips, one to Mycenae and Corinth, and another to Delphi. "At Delphi it was hard not to pray to Apollo for healing," Jack wrote. His early classical education took over as the Greek scholar was finally able to visit places he had only read about for half a century.

Throughout the trip, both Jack and Joy were the life of the party, keeping everyone in stitches. Neither of them felt much pain despite the exertion of travel and sightseeing; everything about ancient sunny Greece delighted them.

Their happiness, however, was not to last. Soon after returning to England, Joy became terribly ill during the night and was taken to the hospital in critical condition. She was dying. On June 20, Douglas, now fourteen, was called home from his boarding school in Wales. The school chauffeur drove him all the way from Lapley Grange to Oxford to see his mother before she died.

No one expected Joy to live since the cancer had spread to major organs. She was taken to the Ackland Nursing Home to die. Yet within a few days, she made another unexpected recovery and, by the end of June, was allowed to return to The Kilns.

Home together again, Jack and Joy made the most of every moment, painfully aware that each night might be their last together. They were so very much in love.

The couple had experienced only three years together as man and wife, but those years had been unbelievably happy. As the end approached, Jack and Joy had one last dinner together at their favorite restaurant and one last drive in the countryside.

The night of July 11, Warnie was awakened by the sound of Joy screaming. He ran down to the common room to find her in excruciating pain. He phoned immediately for the doctor and an ambulance and then called Jack at Cambridge to break the news. Jack rushed to the hospital from Cambridge. Joy died that night with her grieving husband at her bedside.

Once more Douglas was driven home from Wales, but this time to attend his mother's funeral. All the way home in the car, he chatted with Mrs. Cross, the principal's wife, who accompanied him. But on entering the common room at The Kilns and seeing Jack, Douglas could no longer hold back his tears. "Oh Jack, what are we going to do?" he cried, rushing into his stepfather's open arms. Lewis seemed to have aged twenty years. His sunken eyes betrayed the pain he was suffering. Boy and man clung to each other, weeping inconsolably. At last Jack answered the boy's question, "Doug, we'll just have to carry on somehow."

Joy's funeral was held Monday, July 18, at the Oxford Crematorium. Lewis's close friend, Austin Farrer, read the burial service. The marble plaque prepared by Jack in memory of his wife read:

Remember
Helen Joy Davidman
D. July, 1960
Loved wife of C. S. Lewis
Here the whole world (stars, water, air and field
And forest, as they were
Reflected in a single mind)
Like cast-off clothes was left behind
In ashes, yet with hope that she,
Re-born from holy poverty,
In Lenten Lands, hereafter may
Resume them on her Easter Day

CHAPTER NINE

LOVE IS TEARS

A dense cloud of sorrow hung over The Kilns. Joy, the person who had filled the place with hope and laughter, was gone.

C. S. Lewis, to whom thousands had turned for spiritual advice, now found it impossible to deal with his own heart-wrenching grief. Where was the "Joy" he had written about? What had become of his great faith, of his total dependence on God? He couldn't even pray!

Lewis was totally bereft, virtually unaware of even his surroundings, let alone the boys left in his care. It seemed as if God had deserted him, leaving him helpless under this crushing blow.

Often he cried out for Joy, "Come back! Come back!" But he knew that what he wanted was exactly what he couldn't have: the old life, the jokes, the love-making, the little heartbreaking, commonplace things. To say that Joy was dead was to say that all that mattered was gone. Both Lewis and the Gresham boys had expected another miracle for Joy. It never came. She had suffered terribly and then died.

In their grief, it seemed that they had also lost one another. Jack was mourning deeply. Warnie mourned as well, for he had come to love Joy, but he could not handle so much darkness. For years an alcoholic, he now lay in a drunken stupor much of the time. Not long after, David expressed a strong desire to return to America to explore his Jewish heritage and undertake studies at a Hebrew school in Brooklyn. Douglas left as well, returning to Lapley Grange in Wales for his senior year.

Somehow, Jack was able to follow his usual schedule. He continued teaching at Cambridge; it was his duty. To his longtime friends, he presented a brave and cheerful front. Alone at home, however, he frequently broke down, particularly when confronted by Mrs. Miller, the housekeeper, who had taken to wearing Joy's favorite blouses. When he thought of the three happy years of his marriage, Lewis fell into sobs. Grief made him unable to pray or even attend church services.

In December Douglas came home for the Christmas holiday. As a British schoolboy, now a senior prefect, the motherless lad had kept a stiff upper lip. Seeing the agony his stepfather suffered daily, he made every effort to act unaware. When he did break down, he was in Paxford's presence, so it was the gardener who put a comforting arm around the youth and murmured to him not to cry.

Near Paxford's cottage on the grounds stood a small, empty house. Unhappy with his new school in

America, David returned and fixed up the place to live in. The boys took comfort in each other, much as Jack and Warnie had done when they had lost their mother.

For years Warnie had helped Jack with his huge correspondence. Snowed under by grief and alcohol, Warnie now abandoned his brother and moved to Ireland. There he continued drinking heavily until he had to be confined to a Catholic sanitarium near Dublin.

After Douglas graduated from Lapley Grange, it was decided he should keep Jack company at The Kilns. He was entered at Magdalen College School in Oxford, to which he could easily bicycle from The Kilns. Douglas soon came to hate the school, however, finding its students to be "rich and spoiled."

After Joy's death, Bill Gresham had come to England to visit his sons. By then he and the boys had nothing in common. Not surprisingly then, Douglas hardly felt a twinge when Jack later broke the news that Gresham had committed suicide sometime after returning to America. Doug's true allegiance was to Jack, whom he considered the finest stepfather a boy could have.

Despite this, Douglas began skipping classes at Magdalen and finally dropped out of the expensive school, even though Jack had already paid the tuition. Eventually, Doug would go to Applegarth, a "crammer" school, which prepared its students for a general certificate of education. That was all he'd need to gain entrance to an agricultural college, where he hoped to make a career for himself in estate management.

As Jack contemplated his grief and suffering, he felt drawn to write about his experience—his struggle in faith, his inability to think or create, his powerlessness to hold on to any immediate sense of Joy's presence. He felt that he was at the lowest point in a bottomless pit. Remembrances of simple times with his beloved wife delivered the hardest blows—recollections of their favorite walks alone or a joke that only Joy would understand.

In a poem composed after her death, entitled "Joys That Sting," Lewis wrote, "In a life made desolate, it is the joys once shared that have the stings. No one through the years will say the simplest common word in just your way."

One day, the idea came to him of recording his thoughts about Joy, her death, and his overwhelming loss. Written in several partially blank notebooks found about the house, the journal begins with Jack's expression of profound loss and anger at God. "No one ever told me that grief felt so like fear," his first sentence reads. Praying to God when in need, he declared, was to have a door slammed in your face and to hear the "sound of bolting and double bolting on the inside."

Although he never doubted the existence of God, Jack began to doubt God's benevolence. Was God a veterinarian or a vivisectionist—someone who healed animals or someone who dissected animals while they were still alive, for the sake of knowledge? In a feeble attempt to comfort him, friends sometimes offered the worn cliché that at least Joy was in God's hands now. Jack's bitter response was that Joy had been in God's hands all along, "and I have seen what they did to her here."

Yet, the passage of time and the writing of these thoughts showed Jack that "Grief is not a state but a process." The intensity of his pain ebbed and flowed. He could write, with some calm, that already he felt Joy becoming more and more "an imaginary woman." Then the very next entry would be a wretched cry: "O God, why did you take such trouble to force this creature [meaning himself] out of its shell, if it is now doomed to be sucked back into it?"

By the end of the journal, however, he regained his faith in a providential God. Jack began to understand that his unanswered prayers about the meaning of suffering were unanswerable by nature because he was asking the wrong questions. It was as if he were asking, "How many hours are there in a mile? Is yellow square or round?" Being mortal, man cannot see that, in the face of eternity, these are really nonsense questions. All one can really do is surrender to Mystery.

Jack's journal of mourning later became the book *A Grief Observed.* It was first published under the pen name N. W. Clerk, a pseudonym Lewis had used in the past. Only two of his closest friends knew that he was the author. He allowed the manuscript to be published, hoping it might help others who had suffered

an equally devastating loss. The book received a good review in the *Times Literary Supplement* but did not have large sales until published under Lewis's real name in 1964. Today, it is considered one of the finest books ever written on bereavement.

Following Joy's death, Jack's character greatly changed. He became a gentler, kinder man, much less likely to be aggressive during debates and lectures, much less likely to treat other authors harshly in reviews. But he also lost that zest for life that had been so typical of him and now wrote only on the topics of pain and death.

Having passed through the dark tunnel of his wife's pain and weakness, Lewis now had to experience his own.

In June 1961, he began to suffer kidney problems. He experienced difficulty urinating but didn't see a doctor at first. Daily, he felt worse, and his face grew puffy and gray. To his friends, he appeared quite ill.

By the time Lewis finally visited a doctor, his prostate gland was seriously enlarged. He was admitted to the hospital for surgery, but it was discovered that his kidneys were too infected to allow the surgeons to operate. In addition, tests showed heart irregularities. Instead of surgery, antibiotics were prescribed, and a catheter was inserted to drain Lewis's urine into a bag, causing him great discomfort. He was told not to return to Cambridge for the fall term.

No longer well enough to teach, Jack used the free time to reread his favorite books. Friends took him on drives in the countryside, and he never stopped writing new material or reediting former works.

Several times he had to be admitted to the hospital for blood transfusions. Although ordered by his doctor not to smoke, Lewis refused to give it up. "Better to die cheerfully with the aid of a little tobacco, than to live disagreeably and remorseful without," he insisted.

Joy was gone. Douglas and David no longer lived at The Kilns. Warnie had departed for Ireland. Jack was left to the mercies of the Millers, who were skimming money from the housekeeping purse. Never one to keep track of expenses, Jack was unaware of what they were doing.

At the beginning of 1962, his health took an unexpected turn for the better, and he was allowed to teach at Cambridge in the spring term. Over the next holiday, he had a minor operation that permitted him greater freedom to travel. He even planned a trip to Ireland in late July to visit Arthur again. Douglas was invited along to help with the luggage and the driving, as Jack still tired easily, took long naps every afternoon, and at night retired early.

Sadly, the trip never came about. On July 16, Lewis had a heart attack and fell into a coma. At the hospital, he was given the last rites. But a few minutes after the Anglican priest anointed him with oil, Lewis opened his eyes and asked for a cup of tea! He thought he had just awakened from a night's sleep. Lewis remained at Ackland Hospital for several weeks. Even though he did regain some strength, he was not allowed to return home because no one at The Kilns could care for him.

Lewis's friend and biographer, George Sayer, offered to go to Dublin in search of Warnie. Although several people had written Major Lewis about Jack's declining condition, there had been no reply. Warnie refused to open mail with an Oxford postmark for fear of learning bad news.

Sayer arrived at the Catholic sanitarium in Dublin to discover that Warnie was out. The sisters explained that Major Lewis was permitted freedom during the day but had to return by six in the evening for dinner. The head sister assured Sayer that Major Lewis was making progress against his alcoholism and could probably return to England by September. However, she warned Sayer that any word of his brother's condition would certainly throw the Major into depression.

On his return to Oxford, Sayer told Jack the situation. It was obvious to both they would have to come up with another plan.

Over the summer, Jack retained the services of a corresponding secretary, Walter Hooper. Hooper was a slight, pink-cheeked scholar, an Episcopal seminarian from North Carolina. He arrived at The Kilns in the early summer of 1963, at which time Jack was finally allowed to return home from the hospital, although his bedroom was moved downstairs to the "music room." Each morning they tackled the mounds of correspondence that had piled up, with Hooper valiantly taking dictation from Lewis or answering letters as best he could on his own. Hooper also attempted to put Lewis's voluminous writings in order.

By August of that summer, Lewis was too ill to do much. Unfortunately, Walter Hooper had contracted earlier to teach a course at the University of Kentucky and so had to leave in September. He expressed an interest in returning to Oxford the following fall to continue as Lewis's secretary and, ultimately, to write his biography. There were only a few intervening days before Warnie returned from Ireland, sober and eager to help out.

For most of their lives, the Lewis brothers had depended on each other for comfort and friendship. Though they had been separated for a while after Joy's death, they were now together again during these last weeks. Each night Warren went to bed with the dreaded fear, "Will I find Jack alive in the morning?" But there were days when Jack rallied enough to go for a drive or even attend the Inklings' weekly luncheons in Oxford.

There were obvious signs that his brother was failing, but Warnie was unaware of their meaning. Jack fell asleep at strange times. His face was puffy, his appetite gone. Any doctor would have recognized that the end was near, but when it came, no one was prepared.

November was a month that C. S. Lewis always loved. He had written, "Yes, autumn is really the best of seasons and I'm not sure that old age isn't the best

part of life. But, of course, like autumn, it doesn't last."
George Sayer took Jack for a drive in the country, noting Jack's rapt gaze as he praised and adored God in
the beauty of nature.

But when another friend visited The Kilns, he found
that Jack kept falling asleep while they talked. Uremic
poisoning in Lewis's system had affected his brain.
Over the following days, Warnie noticed that Jack slept
most of the time. It was difficult to keep him awake.

On November 22, 1963, Warnie found Jack, as
usual, asleep in his chair. He suggested that Jack go to
bed. Jack agreed and slowly made his way to the music
room. At four in the afternoon, Warnie took his
brother afternoon tea. Jack seemed drowsy and his
speech slurred. Warnie went back to the common
room. He was reading when he heard a loud thump.
He discovered his brother unconscious on the floor. A
few minutes later, Clive Staples Lewis stopped breath-
ing. In just a few days, he would have celebrated his
sixty-fifth birthday.

Douglas and David had been told of their stepfather's failing health. David had been away most of the
time since their mother's death, but Douglas and Jack
had grown close over the years. Now at Applegarth,
Douglas dreaded any news from home, knowing that
his stepfather's death was imminent. On a drizzly
evening, Douglas was in study hall when he heard the
tip tap of a lady's high heels hurrying down the hall-
way. Suddenly, the principal's daughter, Pam Stevens,
appeared breathless in the doorway.

"It's bad news," she said.

Walking back together to the dorm, Douglas asked, "My stepfather has died, hasn't he?"

Pam nodded and wiped away a tear. Her mother, Mrs. Stevens, was waiting in Douglas's room and put her arms around him.

"Jack is dead," she said.

"Yes, I know. Pam told me."

The next day, Major Lewis arrived at the college and drove Douglas back home to The Kilns. A day later, the funeral followed. Overwhelmed by the loss of his brother, Warnie once more drowned his sorrows in alcohol.

Douglas phoned Walter Hooper in the States and asked him to inform the American press of Lewis's death. President Kennedy was shot November 22, 1963, the same day that C. S. Lewis died. The president's assassination overwhelmed the world's news media, and only a short notice of the renowned author's passing appeared in British and American papers.

A small band of faithful friends, the Inklings, a few curiosity seekers, and some neighbors filled the pews in Holy Trinity Church, a typically small country parish. Here Lewis was eulogized in a brief funeral sermon as one of the great Christians of the century. Prostrate on his bed, Warnie was too drunk to attend. With no blood relative present, Douglas and David Gresham followed Jack's coffin to the open grave, a few yards from the church door.

Friends stood around in the still, cold day as Lewis's coffin was lowered into the ground. A single candle on the coffin remained lit until a shovelful of earth fell on the casket, snuffing it out.

The man known to the Christian and literary world as C. S. Lewis had departed the "Shadowlands" of earth for the heavenly home he was confident awaited him.

CHAPTER TEN

A FINAL WORD

So often, after an author dies, his books are not reprinted, and in a few years he or she is forgotten. But Lewis's fame increased year by year.

After his death, Walter Hooper helped Douglas clear out C. S. Lewis's rooms in Cambridge. The two young men transported Jack's voluminous library from Cambridge to The Kilns and then sorted out papers and manuscripts, a Herculean task. Hooper had come to The Kilns to write a biography of Lewis. Access to Lewis's papers, essays, and book manuscripts would make his task easier. Little did Hooper realize that he would spend the rest of his life laboring as editor of, and literary advisor for, both Lewis's published and unpublished works.

The two young men carried box after box from Cambridge to Headington Quarry, checking and sorting reams of handwritten papers. They held in their hands the precious studies of a man whose life had been totally immersed in a search for God and meaning.

Jack's quest had touched many people. Even after his death, his influence spread like ripples on a pond. Courses on the theology of C. S. Lewis were offered at universities, clergy quoted him in sermons, and seminaries of all faiths urged their students to become acquainted with the layman's writings. In addition, the Narnia series became classics adored by generations of children. *The Lion, the Witch, and the Wardrobe* was made into a play, then a ballet, and later both radio and television programs.

In his estate, Jack continued to care for his family. He left funds in his will for his stepsons' education. The bulk of the estate went to Major Lewis during his lifetime, with the residual estate to be divided between Douglas and David on Warnie's death. Douglas completed his studies at Applegarth and then worked in farm management in England and Australia. Today he lives in Ireland, where he and his wife, Merrie, run a support home for unwed mothers and abused women. Douglas has written about his childhood with C. S. Lewis in the lovely book titled *Lenten Lands.* David moved to Switzerland and then was drawn to various faiths and religions around the world. Sadly, the two brothers, now in their fifties, have lost touch with each other.

Warnie continued to live at The Kilns, writing books on French history and struggling with his alcoholism. After his death in 1973, The Kilns was sold. Part of the property was divided into small lots covered with modest homes, with all of the woodlands and the pond placed in a permanent nature trust honoring, among others, Lewis.

In 1984 The Kilns was bought by the C. S. Lewis Foundation of Redlands, California, and has since been fully restored. It now serves as a residential study center for visiting faculty during the academic year and, during the summer, hosts seminars and workshops for students of Lewis's life and works.

As for Walter Hooper, he has since collected, edited, and published many of Lewis's unknown works. He also served as narrator in a documentary about Jack. In 1985, a BBC television production, *Shadowlands*, aired in England. The film told the story of Jack and Joy's late-in-life romance and their trial to the death with cancer. Joss Ackland played the part of C. S. Lewis; Claire Bloom portrayed Joy. The television film later evolved into a very successful stage play and then a motion picture with the same title in 1993. This starred Anthony Hopkins as Lewis and Debra Winger in an Oscar-nominated performance as Joy Gresham. Both Douglas Gresham and the C. S. Lewis Foundation contributed to the film's production.

By 1998 over two million copies of books by C. S. Lewis were being sold annually around the world in many languages. Equally popular are books *about* Lewis, as well as collections of his essays, lectures, and papers.

Lewis was a very private man who spent most of his life in and around the university town of Oxford. He never traveled extensively or sought the limelight. He enjoyed his clubs, his small coterie of writing friends, the Inklings, and, above all, companionship with his brother Warnie. Except for the brief period of 1957 to 1960, Lewis lived the life of a scholarly bachelor.

Then, after six years of an increasingly deep friendship, Joy came into his life like an explosion of a star. For three years, she was his wife, an expression of a fuller life, leading him to new dimensions of body and spirit.

In *A Grief Observed,* Lewis wrote, "There is one place where Joy's absence came locally home to me, and it is a place I can't avoid. I mean my own body. It had such a different importance while it was the body of Joy's love. Now it is like an empty house."

But Lewis did not leave God out of their union. He also wrote, "One thing, however, marriage has done for me. I can never again believe that religion is manufactured out of our unconscious, starved desires, or is a substitute for sex. For those few years, Joy and I feasted on love, every mode of it. No cranny of heart or body remained unsatisfied." He concluded, "If God were a substitute for love, we ought to have lost all interest in him." And, of course, neither of them did. Lewis confirmed, "We both knew we wanted something besides one another—quite a different kind of want."

The marriage of Joy and Jack is one of the great romances of our century. It had all the necessary elements for an opera. Two agnostics found God and then through that discovery found each other. Love and death were the protagonists in their story. But through all the pain and suffering, their faith in God remained firm and secure, their love undaunted. Their faith and love continue to be an inspiration to millions throughout the world.

Clive Staples Lewis was an ordinary man with an extraordinary talent for clarifying the mysteries of religious faith. Understanding his life may help readers and followers get a clearer view of God and his manifestation to humankind in his only Son, Jesus Christ.

Nineteen ninety-eight marked the centennial of C. S. Lewis's birth. Many events commemorating it were held in Ireland, England, and the United States. Perhaps the largest and most splendid were those held at Oxford and Cambridge in the summer of that year. Over eight hundred authors, former students, biographers, and fervent readers of his many books were drawn back to Lewis's much-loved university towns, staying in various Oxford and Cambridge colleges. Morning lectures by renowned scholars and Christian leaders were presented daily in the ornate seventeenth-century Sheldonian Theatre, designed by Sir Christopher Wren.

The afternoons were filled with a choice of courses about Lewis and related subjects. Each evening, a play, reading, or concert was presented in the Sheldonian, culminating in a formal banquet at Blenheim Palace, the birthplace of Winston Churchill.

A main event of the symposium was the release of a special first-class stamp by the British Royal Mail commemorating the centennial of C. S. Lewis. The stamp, as well as a special first-day cover, displayed main characters from the Narnia books.

C. S. Lewis was a man of many interests and talents: a man for all seasons. He will continue to be admired and loved by theologians, lay people, clergy, and children far into the future. Lewis's stalwart faith is perhaps best captured in this characteristic quote from his book *The Weight of Glory:* "I believe in Christianity as I believe the sun has risen, not only because I see it rise, but because by it I see everything else."

FURTHER READING

Books by C. S. Lewis

The Abolition of Man. Collier, 1978.

All My Road Before Me: The Diary of C. S. Lewis, 1922–1927. Harcourt Brace, 1991.

The Case for Christianity. Macmillan, 1989.

Chronicles of Narnia. Macmillan, 1988.

The Dark Tower and Other Stories. Harcourt Brace Jovanovich, 1977.

The Four Loves. Harcourt Brace Jovanovich, 1971.

A Grief Observed. HarperCollins, 1994.

Mere Christianity: Comprising the Case for Christianity, Christian Behavior, and Beyond Personality. Simon & Schuster, 1996.

Miracles. Macmillan, 1978.

Out of the Silent Planet. Macmillan, 1990.

Perelandra. Macmillan, 1987.

The Pilgrim's Regress. Eerdmans, 1992.

The Problem of Pain. Macmillan, 1967.

Reflections on the Psalms. Harcourt Brace Jovanovich, 1964.

The Screwtape Letters. Macmillan, 1967.

Surprised by Joy: The Shape of My Early Life. Harcourt Brace Jovanovich, 1956.

That Hideous Strength. Macmillan, 1990.

Till We Have Faces: A Myth Retold. Harcourt Brace, 1980.

The Weight of Glory and Other Addresses. Macmillan, 1988.

Books about C. S. Lewis

Barfield, Owen. *Owen Barfield on C. S. Lewis.* Wesleyan University Press, 1989.

Dorsett, Lyle W. *And God Came In: An Extraordinary Love Story.* Good News, 1991.

———. *C. S. Lewis's Letters to Children.* Macmillan, 1988.

———. *The Essential C. S. Lewis.* Macmillan, 1988.

Downing, David C. *Planets in Peril: A Critical Study of C. S. Lewis.* Ransom Trilogy, University of Massachusetts Press, 1992.

Duriez, Colin. *C. S. Lewis Handbook: A Guide to His Life and Thought.* Baker Books, 1990.

Gilbert, Douglas and Kilby. *C. S. Lewis: Images of His World.* Books on Demand, 1993.

Gresham, Douglas H. *Lenten Lands.* Macmillan, 1988.

Hannay, Margaret Patterson. *C. S. Lewis: The Man and His God.* Frederick, 1981.

Harries, Richard. *C. S. Lewis: The Man and His God.* Morehouse, 1987.

Holbrook, David. *The Skeleton in the Wardrobe: C. S. Lewis Fantasies.* Bucknell University Press, 1991.

Hooper, Walter. *God in the Dock.* Wm. B. Eerdmans, 1970.

Manlove, C. N. *C. S. Lewis: His Literary Achievement.* St. Martin Press, 1987.

Sayer, George. *Jack: A Life of C. S. Lewis.* Hodder and Stoughton, 1988.

Sibley, Brian. *C. S. Lewis: Through the Shadowlands.* HarperCollins, 1990.

Walker, Andrew, and James Patrick. *A Christian for All Christians: Essays in Honor of C. S. Lewis.* Regnery, 1992.

Walsh, Chad. *The Literary Legacy of C. S. Lewis.* Harcourt Brace, 1979.

Willis, John R. *Pleasures Forevermore: The Theology of C. S. Lewis.* Loyola Press, 1983.

Wilson, A. N. *C. S. Lewis: A Biography.* Fawcett, 1991.